+9.
≥3

# FOOTBALL
## IT'S A MINGING LIFE!
# RICK HOLDEN
## THE AUTOBIOGRAPHY

# FOOTBALL
## IT'S A MINGING LIFE!
# RICK HOLDEN
## THE AUTOBIOGRAPHY

DB PUBLISHING

# Dedication

There are many people who influenced me before and during my career, and many people who put me down too. To all those who put me down - up yours!

The two biggest influences on my life, and by that I mean what I became as a person through football, are my grandfather, who gave me the early encouragement, and Joe Royle, who gave me the liberation to let my character determine my play.

Thanks chaps.

**Rick Holden**

First published in Great Britain in 2010 by The Derby Books Publishing Company Limited, 3 The Parker Centre, Derby, DE21 4SZ.

ISBN 978-1-85983-854-9
Printed and bound in Rzeszowskie Zakłady Graficzne S.A., Poland.

# contents

# Acknowledgements

This book has had the backing of several organizations and people, and I wish to thank the Derby Books Publishing Company Ltd. for undertaking this venture and the *Oldham Evening Chronicle*, the *Watford Observer*, the *Manchester Evening News* and especially the *Halifax Evening Courier* for their cooperation in the use of many of the photographs and for their help in promoting the book. Thanks also to Oldham Athletic FC, Manchester City FC, Watford FC and Halifax Town FC.

I am indebted to all the managers who employed me and believed in me, particularly Billy Ayre and Joe Royle. I have dedicated this book to Joe as, were it not for him, I wouldn't have had the times in football that I ultimately did.

Thanks also to Chris 'Quarfeegle' Kelly, who dealt with the IT side of the operations because I'm a computer moron, and to Stephen 'Melt' Elliott and Jon 'Captain' Hallworth for their memory banks, putting me right on dates and events (I don't know how they remembered it all). Thanks to Andy Ritchie and Andy Kershaw for their kind comments and for taking time to read this tome. I am grateful to my family, who have put up with me, but I have pointed out to my dad, Rodge, that I was all right before 1964 and, therefore, I blame him for everything. Grandpa George needs a special mention for inspiring me in my sports from the early days, and I am truly grateful for that.

Thanks to The Whitehouse Hotel and the Creek Inn, both in Peel, for their support in the launch of this book. If I have missed anyone I am sorry as I can't mention you all, but I have to say that I am lucky in that there are only a couple of people who hate me (and that's their problem). I have some magnificent mates and colleagues. Most of all I wish to thank Dave Moore, my agent and editor, and Oldham Athletic fanatic, without whom this book would have still been in the corner of my study collecting dust.

# Introduction

It was beginning to dawn on me that I was leaving this 'alternative world' and slowly entering the 'real world', but at the same time I was making a move from the 'real world' and entering the 'alternative world.' Not many people do that, do they? What do I mean by that? The world of professional football is not the 'real world' but an alternative world removed from reality, more so these days. Professional footballers live in a protective vista shrouded by money from the reality of the everyday struggle afforded everyone else. It's no wonder that when the shackles are burned and the player is cut loose, like a broken angel, he falls, often to hell. There are examples which are too painful and evidently stark today. Look at George Best and Paul Gascoigne, two of Britain's best two players over the last 50 years, for instance. All the media did, and still does in Paul's case, was slaughter and despair of them. All their former clubs did was keep silent. All these two did was the inevitable. This was an option for me and is for all professional sportsmen and women who come to the end of their careers. We don't have the option of redefined roles like musicians and actors do. We have to become managers, coaches or physios, but it is second best. No limelight anymore, backstage we go. You either cope with your new real world or you remain in an intoxicated, catch-the-past alternative world, grasping, sinking, haunted by memories with nothing tangible.

I had a choice. The best way I could think of coping was to move to a place that was not the real world, but a mirrored alternative world. The Isle of Man is the place. It is unique in the world. Nobody gets it. Nobody understands it. It does not have an identity outside its own (The United Nations do not recognise it as a democracy but it has its own parliament, yet its boys and girls fight in the British Army). The UK hates it. The Labour government withdrew the VAT agreement and the reciprocal health agreement for the Isle of Man residents, yet left the latter in place for residents of Kazakhstan. It does not have an evacuation policy for Manx residents in case of disaster. Yet the Island has fish and chips, real ale, football, secondary schools, in fact everything that the UK has, only, in my opinion, better.

Clearly it was a place worth living in. I decided to move out of England because of the way that life was going, and it would give me a chance to recover while I got over the change. Then it dawned on me that it might help me cope to write it down, shriving myself of my past, if you like. I started writing in 1996 and continued until 2009. I never thought it would get published but more thought of it as a document – at best read by my sons, Will and Alex, and my daughter, Dolly – until Dave Moore contacted me for help with his books. I slowly realised that my story might be worth telling. Yes, I wanted to show every young person that you can make it no matter where you are from and despite all those who tell you that you can't. And to all those fellow players I see toiling like I did, I wanted to say, 'Hey boys, you can survive the move from the alternative world to the real world. You can make it.' I had to keep it together, going into the game as a player from nowhere and recovering when left broken. I did recover. Then I went into it as a physio and as an assistant manager and then was broken again (even after success), but I came through it. So this is not the story about football life as much as life and football. It's not your typical footy autobiography. I don't want that shit, it hides what really happens. The deeper message is that you can laugh and you're allowed to cry but ultimately you must live. Death is no good to anyone, especially those who care.

# Forewords

I spent many a Friday night watching Mick Jones's young Halifax Town team at the Shay with Oldham chief scout Jim Cassell, and when I needed a winger to replace Tommy Wright, my first and only thought was Rick Holden. Rick had moved on to Watford, where things hadn't quite worked out for him, but I had always admired his willingness to work and run at players with the ball. When Rick came to sign, I asked him what he thought he would bring to the team. He responded with a smile and said, 'lots of crosses and extravagant celebrations when I score.' The confirmation of both came very quickly! Football fans everywhere love a winger and Rick was quite simply the best crosser of a ball that I have seen. He soon became the hub of the dressing room, and helped bring a team spirit to the players that I am proud to have managed. Rick, the head prankster, had a sophisticated nickname for some and a wicked one for others, and he was never afraid to hatch a plot or resort to schoolboy humour – it worked! Everyone laughed and trained to their optimum. Saturday afternoons were a joy, and Rick made sure that Saturday evenings weren't bad either. Good luck to Rick, my friend. I await my copy of the book with gentle trepidation. Perhaps the greatest compliment I can pay Rick is that I would have loved to have shared a dressing room with him and to have played alongside him.

**Joe Royle, Oldham Athletic manager (1982–94)**

From the first moment my eyes stared disbelievingly at a tramp (*Professor Holden*) that must have been thrown into the Oldham Athletic dressing room by mistake, to today, Rick Holden has always been the original 'anti-footballer'. Arguably the finest natural winger of his day, and undoubtedly the best crosser of a football I have ever seen, it is possible that he never received the international status his ability deserved due to such obvious eccentricity and steadfast refusal to conform to the stereotypical image of a professional footballer. Picture the footballer of the nineties: bright tracksuit, sharp haircut, bathed in aftershave, thick as a plank. Not for Rick. He was the lead singer of a heavy metal band in football boots, an intellectual in a kindergarten! It was my pleasure (mostly) to be Rick's roommate for the time he was at Oldham and our friendship has continued to this day. My roommate duties were many, from bringing him a cup of coffee and the *Telegraph* on match days, to 'tek me 'ome Captain, am pissed' when we were on tour. On one trip I was berated for the whole week because he was so drunk on the first day that he had fallen asleep in his spaghetti, mouth open. The dental plate in his mouth fell out and his false front tooth was lost in the bolognese. Needless to say, I had to take him home. Next morning I was woken by, 'Captain, where's me tooth?' Explaining the spaghetti incident, I got, 'It's your fault, you giant rooster, you're not looking after me properly.' With no spare tooth, he had the proverbial taken out of him for a week for looking like Steptoe and whistling every time he spoke. Most of the high jinks he got up to cannot be printed, from the outrageous and plain daft to the insulting and sometimes stomach-churningly disgusting antics. These mostly involved me either clearing up after him or apologising to the various offended parties for his behaviour. One thing was certain though, we've never stopped laughing over the last 20 years. On my many visits to the Isle of Man, where Rick now lives, he has carried on where he left off. He's as notorious on the Island as he was in his native North Yorkshire and still as controversial. It's no surprise to me that Rick has written a book of this nature. The book is as he is: straight-talking, opinionated and in-your-face but funny with it. Agree or disagree, love him or hate him, one thing that cannot be denied – he is always very, very interesting!

**Jon Hallworth: Oldham Athletic (1989–97) & Oldham Athletic goalkeeping coach (2001–02)**

# Football – It's a Minging Life!

We had just belched down our last mouthfuls of Sunday lunch and were now entering the post-meal lethargy stage when Melt, showing enormous energy for him, leapt into action and launched the chicken carcass into the back yard. This was the accepted way of dealing with trash in our student house.

'Eh, Melt you twonk, what you f****ing doin', I was going to use that to make a soup.' said Chris, more than a little annoyed. 'Oh yeah, like the others you didn't make', replied Melt.

He had a point. This was always Chris's big culinary plan, which never proceeded past the intention, and the ex-bird would remain festering on the oven for six weeks until the smell became too much, even for us. I went to the window (or more correctly what was left of it, as it had been previously stoved in by Melt's fist in a drunken stupor) to see where the carcass had landed. Normally one of us would hoof it into the corner for the vermin to deal with. To my surprise I saw something small move around the ex-chicken.

'Hey lads, there's a kitten out there and it must be pretty hungry as it's already demolishing the remains,' I said – or words to that effect.

I opened the door, expecting the animal to do a bunk, but no, this was a Leeds cat, it had attitude. He raised his head and calmly entered the house as bold as brass. From that day in November 1986 he stayed with us, travelling the football highway, witnessing many a story and contributing to a few as well. Well, now that he was here what were we going to call him?

At college, we had recently been introduced to one of the most ubiquitous words of all time (it's up there with f**k, it's so good), by a Scottish gentleman called Joe Hulme. He was the captain of the Carnegie College soccer team, and it was obvious that this guy had been involved in a high grade of football as he spoke and organised us with dexterous authority. He had a great influence on my game, mainly through what he said and how he said it, and he had the rare art of being able to issue a convincing bollocking without everyone wanting to either switch off or burst out laughing. He found it almost impossible to complete a sentence without using the word 'minging'. In fact, he found it difficult to construct a sentence without interjecting the word 'f**k' either. He had the full footballer's vocabulary and this, more than anything, else made him a respected man.

In professional football (in Britain), the word 'minging' is the most over-played word we have, and it is used when something is disapproved of or just generally shit. The origin of the word can be found in Scottish mythology and has been used latterly by the great philosopher Rab C. Nesbitt, mainly for the description of an horrendous smell or something that is particularly rancid, e.g. 'That fish smells horrible' is replaced with 'That fish's minging!'

In football, the adjective is used for anything from a player's daft haircut (and there are many examples of this), to a fart (no shortage of these either), and to a bad attempt on goal (enough said). Choosing a name for this orphaned cat was easy, then, as he was undernourished, wet and scraggy, and he probably smelled a bit too. In short he was minging. He became known as 'Minging', and over the years it has evolved to 'Mingan'.

He turned out well and kept going until June 2002. I personally think he looked like a flightless owl, although he used to behave like a dog. We tend to give our pets human characteristics, but he did pick up a few habits off me. He was partial to the odd Chinese meal and used to drink out of pint pots. I hope that sheds some light on the subject and, if nothing else, has given you an introduction to my football mentality.

# one

# From Two Legs to Three

It was nothing like the scene out of *Casablanca* when my dad took off on the 1.30pm to Blackpool. Mission accomplished. I watched as the twin prop, eight-seater buzzed down the runway and escaped against all odds into the great wide open. It all felt rather weird, and yet feeling weird was nothing new for me, and I considered myself a lucky man. With one thing and another, I had descended into a kind of depression brought on, as far as I could work out, by the way I'd been treated in football during the last couple of seasons. It caused me to go out quite a bit, as it was easy to relax and talk about the famous past with a few mates over a pint, and it gave me a sense of importance. The injury that I had sustained, and the fact that I knew it was the end of my career and yet couldn't accept it, meant that I was becoming an isolated agent. I knew I had to create a radical change of scene in order to keep sane and distract myself. Although I wouldn't say that I got anywhere near my Grandpa's achievement of preferring the drunk state to such a degree that he used to announce his sober state when it occasionally occurred, I was beginning to recognise some disturbing behavioural patterns. The reason for this strange declaration will become apparent as we dig deeper into the philosophy of drink addiction, reward and compensation which exists in British football, to the extent that it is almost an incurable disease.

There I was, alone with my family and three cats, which was the purpose for my dad's hair-raising trip. Once again, I had press-ganged him into another all-encompassing 'Rick Holden' adventure, in which field he was by now an expert, and he'd extricated himself from the situation with his usual slow and methodical precision. On booking the flight, I had an interesting conversation with a rather impressively unintelligent girl at the booking office of Comed Aviation.

'I want to book an adult return to the Isle of Man, but there will be three cats to transport as well.' After a dumbstruck pause, the woman countered with, 'And when will you be returning?' I offered up the information, following which there was another pause, accompanied by the annoying tapping sound of info being fed into the computer. 'And will the cats be returning also?' 'Oh yeah, we regularly take cats on day trips, you dumb cluck!' I didn't actually say that but should have done in retrospect. I merely pointed out that, although animal day trips are not out of the realms of possibility in our eccentric country, it was unlikely that, if given the powers of communication, a cat would request such an experience. Such recreation should not, therefore, be provided for them. Mingan has perfected zero recreation – apart from sleeping all he does is wee on the neighbours' bushes. It's funny how something new brings out the daftest remarks from folk. Even the pilot, bless him, said that he would take off at a less steep angle than normal to avoid popping their ears. It hadn't occurred to him that I'd tranquilised the things before we set off to reduce the stress. If you ever get chance to witness the effects of a sedative on a cat don't miss it – it is pure comedy.

On new soil, a son in each arm and the wife carrying the suitcases and cats, we left the terminal building. I had forgotten what it was like here, or maybe I just hadn't paid it any heed. We could have been in a central-American state, with sunshine gleaming on the flags, tall palm trees marching off towards Castletown and weird foreign-looking number plates. They even drive on the wrong side of the road here. Only joking – that's just during TT week! I liked the look of it all.

I suddenly had a cold sweat on my brow and a strange feeling in my gut, similar to being hit in the 'niagaras' from a good length. I put this down to nerves and the fact that I would normally be in a public house enjoying the fine ale. Since 1989 I had conditioned myself to a snifter and something to eat at around 2pm, followed by a couple of hours in the pit. This was a good way of winding down after training, and it did not affect my game. It has been popular recently to declare oneself alcoholic or depressive, and there are a couple of leading Premier League players who have been brave enough to confront their problems head on. I do not fit into this category at all, however, and could not say that I suffered from alcoholism, but it is not a good idea to drink lots of beer when you are a professional footballer.

Right now, though, I had other things on my mind, as I was driving the wrong way around the TT course in 'practice week' and that is not a bright thing to do. At any minute, some leather-clad nutter could fill your space, advancing on you in excess of 100mph astride an exhaustless bike, the noise from which would cause a stampede at a sloth convention. The speed that these things can go at is incredible, and it made my Volvo shudder in its wake. I needed a change of underwear when I arrived at my destination. It's always a good idea to carry a spare pair of crackers with you in case of emergencies and, given the staple diet we used to have at college of three curries a day and a gallon of ale, it became standard issue. Needless to say, I made it to my rented accommodation to recount this story.

The reason for my move to the island was supposed to be a sabbatical in order to get over my injury – I had ruptured my cruciate ligament in February 1996 playing for Blackpool – and to do a bit of physiotherapy in the local hospital, a sort of 'off shore' treat-yourself programme. I had little intention of staying on and, therefore, I viewed it as a holiday. Like many things in life, it did not run to plan, and before I knew it I was sucked in to an eight-to-five job and a financial position that I needed time to extricate myself from. The problem was that I had been offered a contract at Blackpool before my injury occurred, but when the bad news was announced I was very quickly abandoned and left like a broken toy. Clubs bleat on about player loyalty or their perceived lack of it, but so what? The clubs drop players on their backsides as soon as they can, and in my day they showed very little evidence of loyalty. Basically, a player is an asset and nothing more. He is not a person with feelings and a family, but merely a product which can be bought and sold.

I needed time to convalesce and a job to keep the pennies rolling in, and that is all I envisaged my stay as. All my life, I wanted to be a footballer and used to work hard on that dream around the back streets and fields of my home village. The endless hours of joyfully being out of breath, rolling on the grass, looking up at the high clouds and endless drinks of orange cordial were my preparation for life. I never thought that I would do anything else. For me, the world began and finished there. I wasn't about to leave it behind if I could do anything about it, and yet here I was, disappearing across the Irish Sea, doing just that. My belief that I would get back to full strength was so strong that it partly clouded my vision; but then again, I know that one day I will return to the top and succeed again.

# two

## Shay Days

The Monday morning train pulled into Halifax station at 9am. It was late August and quite warm. It had to be, as all I was wearing was an Argentine footy shirt, white arse-hugging shorts and a pair of moulded soccer boots. I didn't own a pair of trainers at the time, so I used my football boots as my principal footwear. I always had done. When I was 13 I demonstrated a new mode of car destruction while wearing the boots. This was by skiing Franz Klammer-style into Ron Matthews's near-side door panel on his new Mazda (you can tell it was the 1970s) from the top of his drive while calling for his son Dave. I was wearing my football boots, minus the studs, and on tarmac this made for a very unstable and tricky combination. The driveway was a one in five gradient (which is bloody ridiculous and is the reason his car was parked at the bottom and not on the incline), and once I reached the top of the slope, gravity and the friction-free surface did the rest. I began sliding down. Unwilling to bail out and fall over and burn my arse or knees as I gathered momentum, there was no way to stop apart from my knees impacting into the side of his car. I'll tell you one thing, it bloody hurt as my shins drove into the undersill of the door. It stung my dad £100 and cost poor old Ron another heart attack. The poor bugger had only just been released from hospital following his first coronary incident and this bit of 'Harold Lloyd' almost got him re-admitted. He climbed back onto his stretcher and asked for 'intensive care please, driver'.

It didn't put me off wearing my new-style trainers, however, and money dictated it. As I arrived in Halifax I was clad in my best recreational clothes, and I thought that I looked good.

Halifax was new to me, although only 20 miles from my home. It was somewhere we had never had the need to visit. Most of my early experiences were of being dragged in the opposite direction into Lancashire to listen to the relatives supping tea on a Sunday afternoon. I walked out of Halifax railway station looking like a tramp out of the *Rocky Horror Show* and picked my way down to the ground half a mile away. People were deliberately crossing the street to avoid me; even respectable Yorkshire yobbos would rather not confront something from another planet on a Monday morning. I arrived at the reception looking like I'd been playing with live cables and introduced myself to the open-mouthed office staff. Other employees came to look at the new exhibit, as if they were staring at a rare animal which had arrived to join the menagerie. 'Er – is Mr Ayre here?' I said. 'Only I've come from Burnley, you see.' Carol, the bewildered secretary, phoned through and I was asked to wait and he'd be along shortly.

While I was standing in the foyer, several players filed past and each one clocked me and disappeared to the dressing room to relate what they had just encountered. They didn't have to wait long, as Billy Ayre arrived and led the extra-terrestrial down into the first-team dressing room, where the first contact was made with the shocked playing staff. It will forever remain with me, the collective look on the lads' faces when I got changed. A fresh-faced youth called Lee Richardson found me some training kit, which I donned with enthusiasm and then, astonishingly, put my mouldies back on, the very same footwear that I had arrived in. There are guppy fish around the world who could learn from the facial expressions of the players when I did this.

Part of the reason for their collective jaw-dropping is that, regardless what level of the professional game they play in, footballers are obsessed with clothes and fashion. Any player who isn't is automatically labelled a 'paraffin' (rhyming slang – paraffin lamp: tramp) and consigned to constant ribbing about his deportment. If it isn't expensive and hasn't got a designer label such as Armani or Versace, then the lads do not want to know. They won't bat an eyelid at paying £500 for a jacket or £250 for a shirt. Years later when I was at Oldham, the Man of the Match award was often a token to spend in Lou Griffiths's clothes emporium in Middleton. The trouble was that the tokens were only worth 50 notes, so to get anything worthwhile you had to hope for a mega season in which you won Man of the Match every time you played. Instead of being outraged at this, though, players accept it as some sort of perverse indication of wealth and stature.

The higher up the ladder you go, the more you spend on clothes, cars, hairdressers and personal accoutrements, and the more skint you will become in the end. More importantly, and this is the crux of the matter, the dafter you will look. One could only stand and marvel at some of the footballers during the late 1980s and early 1990s: they must have had a game plan or an addiction to outrageous dressing. They could send their old suits to the academy for performing arts for extra fancy dress costumes!

Where was I? Halifax Town was a good little club (sadly now down in the Unibond League) and I fitted in very well with my new teammates. Of course, they constantly tried to take the mickey out of me, but it had no effect. After training every day, a vote was held for the yellow jersey, traditionally awarded to the worst trainer of the day and to be worn the next day by the loser. I duly got it for a week, regardless of my performance. The club was more or less solvent, being only £300,000 in debt (compared to Spurs, who in 1987 were up to their necks in millions of pounds). The club has rarely won anything of any real note, and yet it was a well-respected and functioning breeding ground for the fat cats to pounce upon any rat who happened to stand out from the pack.

There was a full compliment of 15 professionals, a few apprentices and Youth Training Scheme (YTS) lads, the manager and his assistant, a youth-team coach and even a physio. The gaffer was Mick Jones, of Notts County fame, and Billy Ayre was his assistant. The youth-team coach was Gerry Brook, who has taken up a form of physical therapy these days and was later to haunt me as an FA drugs tester at Barnsley. The physio was Alan Sutton. He's a smashing lad, and you could occasionally see him directing things at Elland Road on a Saturday afternoon. He was the small guy with a bald head waving his arms about when someone was being substituted, until Dennis Wise sacked him recently. Alan was not a chartered physio – you didn't need to be in those days – but good physios are good physios regardless of their academic background – and I've seen some awful chartered physios in my time. Alan was, at one stage, doing work for Halifax Town, Halifax Rugby League club and Halifax basketball so, as you can see, he was keen (or daft).

I thought that Halifax Town was great, a real club with two men at the helm to run it properly. All the ingredients were in place, from people to do the laundry to pre-season trips, and I was proud to join them. I didn't care much for money, as I'd never had any, and when I did I got rid quickly, usually on fish and chips, the cheapest fuel and, of course, over a bar.

Despite our great team spirit, we followed up our opening-day win over Aldershot with five straight defeats, which placed us at the bottom of the League, and we were faced with the prospect of being the first team to be relegated out of the Football League into the Conference. I had watched the majority of these games and not been given a chance, but that was to change. My first piece of advice to young players would be this: turn up! People cannot pick you if you are not there. I had played one game the previous season for Burnley and had been given the opportunity quite simply because I was there. When I was invited to train with Burnley in 1985, they didn't for one minute expect me to shown up. I did – they were unable to shake me off – and I made the trip down to Leyton Orient with them.

Following a reserve game at Turf Moor, I was told that the gaffer wanted me to travel down with the team on the Saturday. My dad dropped me off outside the ground at 9am and we then endured this hellish trip down to London like some kind of school outing. We stopped off at a hotel outside the capital somewhere and had the ritualistic pre-match meal. I enjoyed the game and the atmosphere immensely, even though we were getting stuffed 3–0. It was the first time I'd been inside any professional football ground apart from Burnley since Elland Road in 1980. With 40 minutes to go, Tommy Cavanagh, the gaffer, told me to get myself warmed up and get out there. After wrestling with my all-in-one shell suit for 15 minutes, I finally ran on armed with all the technical advice usually given by a manager to a youngster making his debut – nothing! I hardly touched the ball and came off absolutely knackered. Still, it gave me an insight into how it was in the Fourth Division, and I knew I could play at this level given more time to get my fitness up to scratch. I had played against many full first teams from the Third and Fourth Divisions at Carnegie over the previous couple of years, and our strong college team had always done well, if not won the games. It gave me a useful yardstick by which to gauge myself.

Halifax were in a bit of trouble, and it was with this in mind that I approached the management in full confidence and holding all the aces. Both Mick and Bill were rather unnerving, though. They both had moustaches in which one could hide several species of small mammal, and both had strong Geordie accents, which made it difficult to follow what they were saying sometimes. My argument must have been convincing, however, and, given the present state of their results, they had little choice but to gamble with me. My first game was ironically against Burnley, the club I had just left following my strange debut the previous season.

Why did I leave Burnley in the first place? Contrary to popular belief, I was not sacked, but rather asked to leave by Brian Miller, the new manager, if I was unable to commit myself to full-time training. Being halfway through my degree course at Leeds, I was hardly likely to do that, especially since they hadn't offered me a contract. Few university students would give up all they had worked for to play football for a Fourth Division side for no money.

During the summer of 1986, when Maradona was running rings around everyone in the World Cup, I retreated to the depths of Yorkshire and played cricket for Saltaire in the Bradford League. I thought that perhaps I had had my chance of playing pro-football and had sacrificed it for my education. I didn't let anyone know my position and my inner thoughts, and I just waited to see what transpired. Then, out of the blue, a phone call came from Billy Ayre asking me to play in some pre-season friendlies for the Shaymen, and I leapt at the chance. Two months later, there I was, about to make my debut for Halifax at Turf Moor. It's funny how things work out.

The debut itself was a strange match in that we totally dominated the game but lost heavily (3–0), paying the price for bad finishing, lapses of concentration in defence and some bad luck. I did well enough, though, thanks to Burnley's right-back Billy Rodaway making me look like greased lightning due to his advanced years. The following Tuesday we entertained Northampton Town at the Shay, who were the early pace-setters of the division, along with Swansea City. We got stuffed 6–3, but as a highlight I scored on my home debut, a right-footed screamer from three yards. As we were waiting in the dressing room for the management, I couldn't help thinking that it was going to be a hard old slog to keep our status as a League club this season if this was the form of things. Bill and Mick arrived, followed by a couple of apprentices carrying two huge trays of lager, and said, 'Have a drink and don't worry, things will work out fine.' This was the beginning of my introduction into reward and consolation through drink.

I returned to college somewhat bemused, had some sleep and then returned to training on Thursday morning. It was a bit quiet and was the same on Friday, with very few clues as to the team for the Saturday home game against Swansea. No team sheet went up, and nobody said a word about the Saturday game. On the Friday night after lectures, I decided that a few pints were in order with my housemates Melt, Chris and Mavoid. I thought to myself, 'I'm probably not in the team after two consecutive defeats, and a few bevvies won't do any harm.'

Unfortunately, I got rather a few more down than I had intended and felt a bit rough the following morning. The only consolation was that I could lie in until 12 o'clock and sleep it off. I turned up for the game feeling okay sleep-wise, though not refreshed and a touch apprehensive that I was to be playing, but I thought I would be left out as I had hardly made a big impact. I had played after 'sessions' before as an amateur – we nearly always did in those days – but it was the norm and nobody made anything of it. Then, like a bombshell exploding in the dressing room, I was selected for the game. The gaffer's pre-match 'troop rousing' concentrated on me and how I had been a breath of fresh air around the place. He told them: 'give the ball to Rick and things will happen!' Pressure or what? I thought, 'I've got to pull myself together'.

A well worn-out saying in the game is 'breathing out of one's backside', used to describe a player going through an uncomfortable period as far as the physical demands of the game are concerned. Players will often declare the fact by confessing, 'Eh, I'm breathing through me arse!' This is what I felt like in the first 20 minutes of the game, but I saw it through and then started to feel good. We soon had the Swans on the ropes. Then, following my corner, Mike Galloway headed in my cross and that was that. We felt liberated and never looked back. The season went on to be a success, and we avoided the ignominy of the drop into the GM Vauxhall Conference by a mile. It was poor old Lincoln City who were relegated, and it was under unusual circumstances. While Lincoln were playing their last game of the season against Swansea, lower-ranked Torquay needed a draw in their final match with Crewe to save themselves. They were trailing by 2–1 in the last few seconds when disaster struck for Lincoln. A dog ran on to the pitch and attacked Torquay player Jim McNichol, causing the ref to add a few minutes to injury time. During this period, Torquay forced the play, and in the last second the dog got up at the far post and headed in the equaliser, saving them from relegation but putting Lincoln down on goal difference. Of course, that last bit isn't quite what happened, but it's the only time a club can say that they were relegated by a dog!

I managed to establish myself in the team and I can safely add that, in retrospect, the next 18 months at Halifax were absolutely glorious. Although not a full-time professional, I was an equal among the pros and they stopped taking the piss, which allowed me to grow and to return any fire with interest.

Halifax Town had a very dangerous feature in that a great deal of our home games were played on a Friday night. This may have been to avoid a clash with other local teams in the hope that a few more fans would venture forth and watch us the Shay. It certainly attracted the 'Brussels sprouts' (rhyming slang for scouts) from all the aspiring bigger clubs, and more importantly gave us a couple of days off over the weekend. Looking back, I'm not sure whether this was a good thing or not, as it enabled the lads to go out on the binge for an extra day and night and consequently reduced the squad's fitness level by about 50 per cent. This led to horrendous training sessions on the Monday if we did not have a game on the immediate horizon. The management duo would suspect that we'd all been out, whether we had or not.

By Christmas 1986 I was still fairly skint and needed some extra pocket money. On returning home from Leeds I decided to do the Christmas post again. This would be the third year on the spin, and by now I was a dab hand at it. I would arrive at the post office at 5am and get handed the biggest parcel bag and mailbag by 'Billy the Post', and off I'd toddle into the blackness. By 7.30am I would return for another batch and by 9am I should have finished. This would then enable me to jump into my dad's car (without asking him) and speed off to Halifax for training. This plan went smoothly until Christmas Eve, when inevitably there was excess post and I had much more to get through. I still had 50 envelopes to deliver when it was time to go, but, sensibly, I had always arranged the round to finish on my street. It was quite simple then: either I would leave them for my dad to deliver, or get Ron Matthews to do it. The latter was easy to achieve as all I had to do was fling them all through his letter box and he would do the rest. The game on Boxing Day was already cancelled due to the frozen tundra masquerading as Halifax's pitch, and I joined everyone in my local pub for a Christmas Eve drink. All was going well until Ron stormed into the boozer, shaking his fist at me, complaining that it had just taken him half an hour to deliver the wrong letters. He knew it was me because he recognised the noise made by my football boots. Obviously, they had haunted him for years. Still, I didn't dent his car this time!

By the end of the season I established myself in the team as a major fixture and, to top it all off, I was awarded the Player of the Season by the fans, of which I was very proud. What a great day the final match of the 1986–87 season was. It was also a day of hilarity and deep embarrassment, and one that should be a lesson to any young player.

Mick Jones had by this time left to join Peterborough United, for what reason I'm not quite sure. Maybe he thought that it was a better bet than poor old Halifax. His soul was more impoverished for the move, however. It was the Posh who provided the opposition on this day and, before the match, Mick had presented me with my trophy and the token bottle of whisky. (If you take a close view of the picture taken at the time, I look like I've just swung down from the trees to collect the prize). We won 1–0, and I had launched in the winner to set up a perfect day, as later it was our annual awards dinner at Carnegie in order to honour the final-year students' academic and sporting achievements. My friends Melt, Mavoid and Chris came to the game, and following that they joined me, first in the players lounge for a swift gargle, then around Halifax on a whistle-stop quality-control tour for Webster's brewery. At around 7pm we boarded the train and set off for Leeds. There we were, full of the joys of youth, going to our ball armed with a full bottle of whisky, which, like college idiots, we drank. Although this is not a vast amount between four strong lads, it is not a good idea to pour it onto several previously imbibed pints. Also, following a game, when blood sugar is low and the metabolism on red alert, this can have disastrous effects on the system. We kept up the assault on the sauce when we arrived in the student bar, so by the time we came to be seated, I was fairly well charged up! My partner for the evening, and, as it turned out, my future wife, gave me one of those down-the-nose sideways glances of abject disgust and did what she has become very good at over the years – ignore me! The evening's dinner seemed to pass without incident, but it was only the calm before the storm.

The ceremony started and the opening speeches went on for about half an hour before we came to the main event. 'And now, to our outstanding sporting achievement award, which this year goes to one of the most yeah yeah waffle blah who has full colours for cricket and football and has also become a permanent feature in the Halifax Town side, and indeed who scored the winner today. Ladies and gentlemen: Rick Holden!'

At this point we have to take Melt's word for it, but I know it's a fairly accurate account of things because my wife Jean still refuses to comment on it. Apparently, when called upon to receive the award and make my way up to the stage, I over-balanced due to the electrolytic mixture in my cerebral arteries and fell backwards in 'reverse superman' pose onto a table of eight behind me. The resultant explosion of glasses and crockery was enough to wake up the lecturers on their table and naturally caused chaos for around five minutes. I was helped to my feet and then escorted from the building, like Roger Banister after the four-minute mile, with an arm draped over my assistant's shoulders, never to return again! There is a lesson in this for all of us, and it's certainly not the thing to do at the annual PFA awards if you can avoid it.

In the summer I was summoned to Billy Ayre's presence in order to put pen to paper for a full professional contract. I was offered the staggering sum of £125 per week. This was better than nothing, and I had very little choice but to sign as I had nothing else planned and didn't fancy getting any other type of job; the type of jobs I had done up to that put me off somewhat. I had always wanted to be a professional footballer and I wasn't going to miss this opportunity, even if the money wasn't exactly brilliant. I figured that, if I worked hard enough at my game, the rewards would come. Until pre-season began I kept myself busy playing cricket and working at Webb's chicken factory at Cross Hills. What an eye-opener that was. During the summer of 1985 had I landed a job in a cheese factory at West Marton Dairies just outside Skipton, which mainly consisted of stacking huge lumps of cheese onto pallets. After a week or so I was transferred to the effluent plant as they had developed a problem with the . . .er effluent!

If you are familiar with effluent plants, then you'll recognise the rotational filters which spray water out onto a grid system as the whole thing spins round. My job was to sit in the middle of the filter, rotating around with it and, when I saw a hole get blocked with gunge, crawl down the arm and release the blockage with a wire brush. I thought this was the world's worst job, but the job at Webb's was even worse. My first task at the chicken factory was folding the wings back on recently chopped-in-half breasts and placing them on the conveyor belt, which transported them into the freezer room. In fits of stultifying boredom, wings would be bent into all manner of positions, the favourite being the Nazi salute. When half a dozen emerged frozen at the packing plant paying homage to Adolf Hitler, the foreman would come racing out to bollock the troops. Promotion from this point was to the freezer room itself to stack the frozen birds onto pallets. This gave me an insight into what it could be like in 200 years time when men are mining for raw material on Mars. It wasn't just through the freezing temperature that I received this enlightenment, it was from the people who worked in there, too. They were definitely strange, as if from another planet, and I could only surmise that they had been affected by the extreme cold.

The ambient temp was -30°C . For those who haven't visited Antarctica, that is bloody cold – so cold in fact that we had to wear special suits and have a 10-minute break every hour to defrost. One of the ways of alleviating the boredom in this martian landscape was to organise a game of football or ice hockey with a full frozen chicken. The ball or puck used to fly along the floor extremely well due to the amount of ice coating the outer surface of the unfortunate bird. This game was also interrupted by the irate and stressed foreman.

Finally, I was transferred to 'live hanging on', where I was forced to become the Grim Reaper of the poultry world. Quite simply, my task was to take the birds out of the boxes, hang them upside down on sheckles by their feet, and propel them towards their doom. I was chief executioner and it gave me a few nightmares, I can tell you. The first problem was the flapping about of the panic-stricken bird. Claws and beaks everywhere would ensure a few spikings along the way, resulting in local infections of the fingers and thumbs. Obviously, the stench was awful. The mixture of warm blood and shit, the smell of death I called it, was so overpowering and hideous that when you first encountered it you retched in a reflex action. One had only to walk around the corner to the 'hanging room' and the smell would hit you like a wall. As the birds were transported along the gantry, they were dipped in a water tank carrying an electric current, which stunned them before they approached a three-way switch-blade knife system which removed the heads of the poor foul. The birds literally shit themselves and it went everywhere, including onto the workers, and that, my friends, is not pleasant. So there you are: my three years of summer work to repay education debts mainly involved shit, which is why I said it was quite useful in that it was more than enough preparation for the trials of pro football. They could throw what metaphorical shit they wanted at me in the game, but it was never going to replace the real thing.

We had an enjoyable pre-season visiting the glamorous North East. Billy Ayre was from there, and he had the obvious old contacts in the game. Teams like Peterlee, Seaton Carew and Whitby Town were our opposition and provided us with the usual tough amateur battles against the pros. I can distinctly remember one of our lads, Wayne Allison, crumbling to the core at the thought of training on the beach at Seaton Carew. It was absolutely freezing and not his idea of spending time on a beach. His personality was more suited to the Caribbean. I, conversely, had been training in the fridges at Webb's chicken factory and doing the Christmas post in the frozen wastes of North Yorkshire. We remained remarkably incident-free during this period, apart from capsizing a couple of boats on the River Wear in Durham while on our afternoon off, but that was mainly Mick Galloway's bad seamanship.

The season started off well, if not spectacularly, and by Christmas we were in the play-off positions. Halifax Town were starting to attract the attention of the big guns, such was the excitement that our young side was generating, and it wasn't long before the inevitable happened and the side was dissected and scattered to the four winds. Mike Galloway was sold to Hearts, while Dave Longhurst made the slightly odd move to Northampton Town. They were both good players and great characters, but I thought that they should have been held onto a little longer and sold to larger and more ambitious clubs. This may seem a little harsh on Hearts, who played in Europe that season, while Northampton had just won the Fourth Division and thus were trying to strengthen their squad, but it was just the way I felt. Incidentally, Mike Galloway went on to play for Celtic, which shows his personal ability and the latent skill hiding in the Halifax team at the time.

One evening I was given a very poignant lesson as to the harshness of professional football. Our left-back was a college colleague of mine from Carnegie called Frank Harrison. He had been at Middlesbrough years before but then had decided upon the academic route when things hadn't quite worked out for him at Ayresome Park. Billy Ayre, like many Nationwide Conference and lower division managers and scouts then, had gone to watch the college scene and was at my college when he spotted this terrific player swanning around on Wednesday evenings, along with another excellent player, Mark Fenton, a goalkeeper also playing for Harrogate Town. Frank was signed and was left-back, while I was on the left wing. We were playing at home against Colchester United when, out of the blue, an over-the-top challenge went in against Frank and the crack of broken bone snapped through the cold night air of the Calder Valley. Retribution, in the guise of a challenge on the perpetrator by our captain, Mr Brown, was swift, but it wasn't enough. Frank never really recovered and eventually slipped away and missed his chance to play at the highest level, which I'm sure he would have done. That's football, I'm afraid, and it is only the luck of the draw when it comes to incidences like this. It makes you realise just how fragile a sporting career is. Frank may have had his degree to fall back on, but that was no consolation for him. He wanted to become a top-class professional footballer, not hobble around with an academic qualification under his arm. Frank was a defender with that awfully rare habit of being able to pass the ball to one of his own players.

Let me cheer the scene a little with a wonderful tale from the Shay's halcyon days. Phil Brown, the captain of the side, shared a house with an eccentric Scotsman called Russell Black, who happened to play up front for the team. Blacky was keen on making up his own idiotic poetry, among other things, and his physical quirks matched the verbal ones. Blacky was the archetypal player, who had all the vices to some degree or other, and that alone should have ensured that he played a lot higher than in his brief spell at Sheffield United. For some reason I cannot recall, I had found myself at Black and Brown's residence prior to a game and discovered it wall to wall with women. All was calm, and we were just chatting quietly when the phone rang. In strode Brown, like a butler, to answer the call. 'It's for you,' bellowed the butler, with his neck craning towards the stairs. 'I'm 'aving a shite man, who the f\*\*k is it?' replied Black, like a true country gent. Several of the ladies had gone pale at this response. 'It's Mandy, your girlfriend,' retorted Brown, who by now was laughing, as he knew that this was not the kind of information that Black would want divulging. There was a pregnant pause, followed by a few muffled expletives. The sound of descending footsteps materialised in the stark-bollock form of the man in question and was met by gasps of incredulity from the players and silent pallor from the female contingent. Bold as brass, he traversed the room, treating everyone to a full close-up of his wedding tackle, and it was not until he had walked past us all into the corner of the room to pick up the phone that the full horror of the atrocity hit us. In order to arrest his peristaltic nether movements, he had wedged a full toilet roll between his arse cheeks. I can honestly say I had never seen anything like it in my three debauched years at Carnegie College, when we would have made *The Young Ones* look like angels, and I have not seen the like since. The upshot of the tale is that following the evening game, in which he didn't score, he did manage to score afterwards with one of the young ladies who had witnessed the outrage earlier in the day.

Back to the main theme: we stuttered towards Christmas, and then things began to change for me personally. I was like a pig in muck, and I wished that it could have gone on forever, but deep down I probably knew it wouldn't, couldn't and shouldn't. If a person has ambition and a modest amount of intelligence then there is a time limit for how long you remain in a place or a job or situation. The exception to that rule is if you are at the top, and then there is no place else to go except sideways to another challenge. That is the morphology of football and many other businesses. Things are very cut and dried in football, but that's the way it is. You have to accept it and adapt, and that is what I eventually had to do at Halifax.

# three

# Watford – Nothing But a Pot to Piss in

The Halifax Town days were wonderful, or in football speak, a 'different class'. Halifax is a very friendly club, and they embraced me once they got over the initial shock. Having travelled to every football club in the land several times to enjoy their hospitality, the one thing that strikes you is whether the club has any of those over-officious guards securing the entrances to public access as if it were personal crown jewel-like property. Halifax does not. The world and his mum could get into the players' lounge after a game and yet there wasn't any trouble. People just accepted that this close contact with their heroes was par for the course. When I went further up the ladder, I was amazed at the officialdom in the game. I was just a footballer after all, and yet at places like Arsenal, West Ham, Spurs and Man City they used to protect the access as if the people inside were something important. We need security from some of the idiots, but when it's your family – mums, dads, children, grandparents – asking for tickets for them to gain entrance when they are with you was taking the piss and never won any friends. Perhaps it is purely a reflection on society, and it showed the difference in trust between so-called big clubs and small family clubs. Sadly, it is getting that way with small clubs now.

The news of a move to Watford crackled across the rumour airwaves. There were always plenty of 'Brussels' at the Friday evening games: managers came to Halifax to witness the raw meat on display for themselves. This was the advantage of playing Friday night football – no self-respecting gaffer would pass up on the opportunity to see a first-team game on a Friday night. Fourth Division football was always bargain basement territory for the big boys, and it was another excuse for the manager to get out of the house and pretend he was busy. Halifax had a good young team (and I seemed to be attracting some attention), with the exception of Paddy Roach, who was possibly reliant on WD40 to get him through a game and who would punctuate the show with the occasional flash of brilliance. Paddy, incidentally, was always allocated the back seat of the coach so that he could blow his cigar smoke out of the back skylight on the way to the games. I was suddenly dragged into Billy Ayre's office – you don't enter or get asked to go in, you are metaphorically dragged in or pulled in – and I was informed about Watford's interest, as if I didn't already know (although I thought he was going to give me a bollocking about something). Watford had put in an offer of £125,000 and was I interested? Of course I was. I had relatives in the area and Watford had pummelled their way into the First Division. It didn't put me off that they were attempting to break the record for consecutive League defeats and that the prospect of them remaining in the top flight with just 10 games left was rather unlikely.

I felt saddened at having to leave Halifax, and I wondered why I couldn't have stayed and been paid more in order to try to move the club and myself further up in the world. But that's the way in the footy arena: the flash of the pound signs is often the beginning of the end, and clubs will cash in if they can make these huge profits we see today. Halifax paid the ultimate price several seasons later and slipped to the verge of obscurity, though by some miracle they keep going, still repeating their mistakes by selling their top striker to Fulham. Oldham are in the middle of paying that price and oblivion beckons for all clubs if they don't achieve some stability.

The prospect of mixing with the alien southerners was one thing, but supping their flat ale was about as inviting as a pile investigation. Would I go down to Watford and talk to the manager Steve Harrison and see what I thought? I hadn't been to Watford since my dad used to take us in a clapped-out Dormobile on endless journeys from Skipton to Hemel Hempstead in searing heat to visit our cousins, Andrew and Martin. I knew it was down there somewhere, but hadn't appreciated just how far down into the pit it was. London Bridge is only 20 miles from the centre circle. I set off from Leeds down the M1 in my clapped-out Mini – it's not until you're in a Mini with a top speed of 60mph that you realise what a horrendous artery the premier route in our country is. Huge wagons, like moving tower blocks, ploughed past me, relentlessly throwing buckets of water on to my windscreen and making the car shudder with the vibrations. At one stage the spray was so violent that it was hitting the windscreen more quickly than the wipers could flick it off. Consequently I had to drive with my head out of the window to make sure I didn't become a statistic. By the time I reached Watford I was tired and wet through; however, the early spring sunshine was making a comeback as I pulled into Vicarage Road and I thought it was a good omen. My dress sense hadn't altered much since my arrival at Halifax Town two years earlier, and, added to that the knackered grime-yellow Mini, which backfired on arrival due to the cracked exhaust which I'd tied up with a Burnley scarf, and my drowned-rat appearance, and you begin to see why Mr Harrison thought the plumber had arrived to fix the boiler. When it dawned on him that I was his latest big signing, he was speechless and his eyes glazed over as he searched his memory for a similar situation in order to act appropriately. Failing to find one, he led me to the reception where I was introduced to a large lady called Sylvia, who looked like the giant Womble, Madame Cholette, and he disappeared for about five minutes. Madame Cholette talked about nothing and gave me a couple of Elton John signed albums, and I wondered whether she always did this for the new players. Was it part of my signing-on fee, or did she just feel sorry for this scruffy northern lad with shaggy wet hair? Harrison reappeared and led me to a bathroom suite, where he presented me with some shaving tackle, a hairbrush, some shampoo and a towel. When I caught sight of myself in the mirror, I understood why. As I reached the end of my army recruitment ablutions, the manager entered again. I was then led away to his office, where he presented me with some Watford-issue trousers and a shirt, tie and jumper. To cap it all, he removed the blazer from his back and put it on me. We then descended into the bowels of the club, where I was introduced to the physio, Billy Hayles, and his ancient assistant, Pat Malloy, from Barnoldswick, and Ernie and Tom Whalley (pronounced Wally).

'This is Rick Holden from Halifax. This lad can cross a ball!' said the gaffer. 'Yeah, but how many f\*\*kin sit upsies can he do boysies, eh?' gabbled Tom, who then stood up, punched himself in the guts several times like an outraged baboon, and grabbed my cheek and wobbled it about so that my mouth made a sloshing sound. Confused and utterly dumbfounded, I then got changed and went for my medical, looking like one of those old blokes you see dressed in jacket, shirt, tie and trousers, offset with a pair of trainers because they've got corns. In my opinion, I looked worse now than when I arrived. At least before I could have passed for a scruffy workman; now I looked like a trampy old bloke going to collect his pension. I passed my medical, although I failed the fashion test, and then I returned to the depths to see my new gaffer. I signed a four-year contract. I had to, I supposed, if I wanted to make it. If I did well, he said he'd review it. I had gone from £225 a week at Halifax to £450 per week with £50 appearance money per first-team match. I received a signing-on fee of £10,000, split into three payments, one payable now, and the others in July 1989 and July 1990. I was given a £2,000-per-year loyalty bonus to make the signing-on fee up to the usual 10 per cent of the sale. It was very nice, and not bad for those days.

After a busy day I retired to Hemel to my Uncle Dave's, where Beryl had cooked her usual, immaculate five-course meal, and we were joined by my cousins, Martin and Andrew. After dinner, barely able to walk through food overload, we retired to the Leatherbottle in Leverstock Green to sample some of the latest expensive flat ale. I saw Kevin Richardson and Wilf Rostron, but they didn't recognise me. Why would they? Halifax hadn't been on television since, well, never, I think. Kevin had just left Watford for Arsenal, following a disagreement with Dave Bassett in Sweden, probably over something ridiculous like the ground speed of the Tasmanian swallow. He was a clever player, who had been the star of the show in Everton's defeat of Watford in the 1984 FA Cup Final and played on the left wing, where I was trying earn my living.

The next day I went and trained with the lads, being introduced to them as the replacement for John Barnes. I joked that I didn't look a bit like him. They just laughed, and I laughed too. Training was taken by Tom Whalley, with the gaffer interrupting with ranting outbursts. Tom was unbelievable and also, for that matter, unintelligible. When we'd met the day before in the downstairs management room, I'd given him the benefit of the doubt. Twenty minutes into the warm-up on my first day of training, I was convinced that this was a seriously strange and eccentric man. Training was great, I loved it, but I hadn't understood a word he'd said. He was the first and only man I've met who talked in plurals and interjected Welsh words without realising it. I looked around, and what made it funnier was that the rest of the lads seemed oblivious to it. The stuff he was coming out with was outstanding. A year later I realised why this was – they were brow-beaten and defeated. Stunned and yet impervious, the session never changed. 'Rightis ladsis, stretch your backsis legsis offsis – good ladsis?' was his favourite. I tried to point out that I didn't possess any back legs, just arms and legs but it made no difference. His other classic pieces were the mixing of cliches and metaphors to hilarious effect.

As I've already pointed out, football talk/speak is unique, chiefly consisting of the words 'minging' and 'f***ing', and with as much rhyming slang as you can get into any one sentence. It is not cockney rhyming slang, however, it's football rhyming slang, which is basically words selected to have some significance with soccer. For instance, a cup of tea is a 'Franny Lee', or if you're older a 'Bertie Mee', and classics such as 'Hampstead Heaths' (teeth) become 'Adrian Heaths', and so on. It's merely playing around with words because of boredom. Similies are popular too, but only clichéd ones. Poor old Tom could never get to the bottom of all this and, consequently, gem after gem would emerge in semi-Welsh plurals. I loved to listen out for them. My favourite was his use of 'current bun' (the sun), for his head, as in, 'Over 'ere mate, on my current bun!' One morning he pulled me over to one side during training, after we had signed a former apprentice and my very good friend Lee Richardson from Halifax Town. Tom said that since I'd been down here for a year or so and that, as I knew him well, I was to show him the ropes and look after him because Lee was 'as green as the ace of spades'!

I remember one incident very clearly, which I put down to gross ignorance at the time, but with the benefit of hindsight may not have been. Perhaps I am getting softer in my old age, or softer in the head, but I may have the root cause of Tom's display. He originated from north Wales, Caernarvon to be exact, and his first language is Welsh. Whenever nervous or excited, or in Welsh company, he would lapse into his pidgin English/Welsh mix, which sounded like he was trying to gargle a tub of frogs. At Newcastle airport, we were waiting to be flown home in our six-seater World War Two bi-planes after being single handedly thrashed 3–0 by a youthful Paul Gascoigne, a game in which, by some miracle, according to a match magazine, I got Man of the Match award for Watford. Not really having anyone to talk to, I slid across to enjoy Tom's company. He was holding court with two other Welsh representatives, Iwan Roberts and Malcolm Allen, in their native tongue. I stood there for a few minutes wondering if they were going to bring me into the fold and revert to English, or at least for one of them act as an interpreter, but they didn't. I got embarrassed and slipped away. I wasn't really bothered that they completely blanked me, but I never forgot it, and it put me on my guard. The fact was that Tom made more sense to me in Welsh than he ever did in English.

The final piece in his personality jigsaw, which elevated him into the 'bizarre legends' category and completely set off his character was a huge, ballooned right knee, which manifested itself into an outrageous limp. Looking back now it must have been an old knee replacement that he'd worked almost to the point of metal fatigue. With each step he took, he looked as if he was about to collapse into an armchair. He would recover using an uplifting jerk of the arms. After all this, though, I liked Tom and thought he was a good bloke. His quirky eccentricity is what is required in football and, on top of that, he has done great things for Watford and Millwall, especially with the kids.

I digress again. Following training on the Tuesday morning, which was so intense that I am sure that, if accurate records had been kept, I would have broken the qualifying time for the Olympic 1,500 metres, I jumped into my super Mini and sped back up the MI to Leeds. It was like being on a skateboard with a lawnmower engine.

Three hours later – which is good going – I was in the great city of Leeds and, having picked up my gal, was heading to Skipton. I got thinking about Skipton and its facilities. I was born at Cawder Gill hospital in the area, now sadly closed down. It is a busy market town which appears in the *Doomsday Book* and has had some significant roles to play throughout history, particularly during the Civil War, when it was a Royalist stronghold. Famed for its castle and market, it champions itself as the 'Gateway to the Dales'. My childhood back garden, the open-plan valleys of Wensleydale and Wharfedale, are descended upon every year by the flat cap and caravan brigade, and the backpackers and real ale societies. Funny types these ramblers. When scaling something like Embsay Crag in summer, a 1,300ft Dales molehill, they will dress as if they're about to ascend the north face of the Eiger, while locals skip past them in plimsolls and T-shirts. Then in winter, when it's so cold that even the yetis have abandoned the hills and come down to the local for a warm-up and a whisky, the nutters will be out there finding new and interesting ways to get lost in order to test the skill of the Dales' rescue team! I thought some more, and it occurred to me as we began our descent into Otley what a weird and wonderful place this area is.

It is essentially a crossroads or stage coach station, nestled in the bottom of an old lake in the outpost of the West Riding in the Aire Valley on the border of Lancashire, and that is why the market appeared. Lots of people from all over the country constantly pass through it, stop to buy things, look around the local tourist spots, and yet nothing ever happens, nothing ever changes and nothing ever gets done. The mark of any town worth its salt is whether it has a decent football team competing in the pyramidal system. Skipton does not. What it has is a local league (the Craven District Football Association League), in which three teams, Skipton LMS, Skipton Bulldogs and Skipton Town all compete, fluctuating from crap to average. It must be the largest town population and catchment area in England not to have floodlights and a decent town team.

One thing that I am often confronted with in the Isle of Man is the following scenario: 'Our Johnny was a good player, he went away for trials, but the travelling was too much, he got homesick so he didn't make it. But he was good, he could have made it.' Do they think I was spotted because the amateur pitches in Yorkshire are lined corner flag to corner flag with scouts making copious notes about the lads? Bollocks! I'd have still been playing for Skipton BR (LMS) now if I hadn't got off my arse and done something about it. Of course I had help. We all need that, but the spark must come from within and the desire must be self-made. Skiptonians who give me little Johnny stories have no excuses. They do not have a 70-mile stretch of water to negotiate, all they have to do is jump into their cars and drive. Undoubtedly the single biggest factor that has prevented lads making it into the big Leagues from the Isle of Man is the isolation caused by the briney barrier. Incidentally, those who broadcast the argument that you have to make it young are also talking bollocks!

One of Skipton's best features is that it has plenty of boozers and, like most places, had dozens more once upon a time which have sadly been closed down. It's a crying shame and rocks me to the core when someone says, 'Oh yes, the estate agents Turpin and Price. Their office used to be the Ship Inn.' I mean it's bad enough that it closed down, but bloody tragic it ended up as an estate agents. One pub that will hopefully never close down is the Black Horse Hotel, which was where Jean and I were heading for then. Recently it has been refurbished to the tune of several million pounds, but has maintained many of its original features such as its three-feet thick pillars and huge roaring fire. Situated at the top of the high street, next to the castle and church, and directly opposite the equally antiquated Red Lion, it is steeped in history. Off the cellars are underground vaults and passages which connect up to the aforementioned buildings. It was a subterranean link for the nobility and priesthood to gain access to a late-evening snifter without being spotted by the riff-raff. Waiting for me in the Horse were my excited family and friends. We pulled onto the cobbled sets and three seconds later I was halfway down a pint of Taylor's Landlord, a quality drink for a quality occasion in a quality town! I announced the news about signing for Watford and that I was to make my debut against Everton at home on Saturday. It was a proud moment for my admirers, who'd seen me play football since day one and followed my progression to the highest level. One man, Martin Greenwood, was amazed – prior to this piece of information he had thought that my sole contribution to civilisation was my ability to drink, telling my dad, 'Bloody hell! I thought I could sup, but your lad, I never seen 'owt like it!' Michael Windle, prince of slowness and master of the understatement, was only concerned that Kenny Dalglish hadn't matched the offer and my Yorkshire soulmate, Barry, part of the Black Horse furniture, was rendered speechless. Barry was the caretaker at Craven College of Adult and Further Education and had become a close friend of my father's, the Head of Centre of the establishment. I had always liked the connection, the boss and the caretaker being close buddies and meeting up for a pint or six in the Horse after work. Conveniently, the college is next door to the Horse and so, if I couldn't find my dad, or if anybody else noticed his absence for that matter, then we would know where to find him. Barry was central to my footballing development because whenever he came back to our house with my dad after they'd been turfed out of the local, usually the Cavendish Arms in Embsay, I would always get to watch *Match of the Day*. When dad went for a pee I would take the opportunity to sneak down the creaky stairs, say 'Hi' to Barry, and then hide behind the curtains by standing on the windowsill. From here, I got a bird's-eye view of the game and I can recall every piece of action from the seventies. You name it, I saw it. So what did I want to be if I grew up? You guessed it.

Back to the Horse. It was about 2am and no one gave a toss. No trouble about a late gargle here, and that's how it should be and how it is in the rest of Europe. I had a good lie-in the next morning. I needed it because at 6.30am on Thursday morning I was in that Mini again dropping Jean off at Water Lane in Leeds and off on another M1 epic. Professional footballers are hardened drivers and subsequently think nothing of driving 200 miles to training. Many players go into the pub trade after their career bites the dust, but they could quite as easily become sales reps or long-distance lorry drivers. Dave Robinson, who played at Halifax and shot to fame by getting us ejected from our hotel in Magaluf with his methods of watering the plants in the hotel reception, became a long-distance lorry driver.

By 9.30am I was passing under the road to Hell and heading to the training ground at Stanmore. Watford didn't have the luxury of owning its own training complex back then and therefore had to hire North London Polytechnic's playing fields, which are so huge that it would take my old teammate Kenny Jacket half a day to run around it. Mind you, poor old Kenny was so hopeless at long-distance running that when we used to do cross-country in Cassiobury Park we'd have to send out a search and rescue team to bring him in. God only knows how he used to get through 90 minutes on a Saturday. It didn't seem to affect him and he put in many outstanding and energetic performances for Watford over the years, but if he'd been examined by an exercise physiologist he wouldn't have been passed fit to play bowls. At 12.30pm I was being interviewed by the *Watford Observer*, and by Friday morning I was big news in the southern tabloids: 'Young winger from up north to make debut against Mersey giants.' Friday's training session consisted of another of Tom's SAS induction-course warm-ups, followed by something I'd not come across before – pattern of play. Out of a squad of 16 the gaffer bibbed up the team of 11 for Saturday's match and had the remaining five act as defenders. Prior to going into this kind of session, we would normally be subjected to a soliloquy of epic proportions while we stood around in discomfort as our sweat turned cold on our backs. These addresses would sometimes last as long as 20 minutes, and that was the odd thing. There would be no way that Mr Harrison could get away with this in Halifax because it was too damned cold – the lads would have been keeling over with hypothermia – but in Watford it was warm, like another country, although standing around letting the sweat congeal on your back was an open invitation to catching a chill. I couldn't get over how warm it was in the south in mid-March, whereas in the frozen north we'd still be expecting some harsh weather.

During the speech Harry would bring Tom in by asking, 'In't that right Tom?' But Tom had glazed over like the rest of us and this invitation would catch him unawares. 'Er… that's right gaffer. You've justs got to er get in to 'em, that's right Gaffer,' which had a profound effect on us all. Sometimes during the pattern of play, the manager would line the 11 due to start up against no opposition at all, the invisible man 11 or playing against the dustbins as we would call it. 'Right. 'Keeper gets it and off we go,' or, 'Our throw-in full-back gets it and play,' were the usual modes to begin with. Tony Coton would collect the ball, usually booted to him from Harrison in such a manner that I was convinced his leg was going to fly off, and throw it out to Nigel Gibbs, the full-back. 'Good, good,' said the gaffer. Gibbsie would then pass it inside to Gary Porter at inside-left, 'Good, good!' Gary would slip the ball into the centre-forward, big Dave Bamber. 'Good, good, good!' Big Dave would roll the ball to me and it would bobble under my foot and go out for a throw-in to the invisible 11. 'F\*\*kin' 'ell! We can't even beat the dustbins, eh Tom!' 'That's right gaffer. I mean we've got to get in there.'

Put yourself in my position. There I was one minute at Halifax Town in the Fourth Division, a club run very professionally by Mick Jones and Billy Ayre, but not without its problems. Suddenly I am transferred to Watford of the First Division thinking, 'I'm really going to learn something new with these guys'. And what do I end up with? A scene out of *Monty Python*. Don't get me wrong, Steve and Tom were very professional and left no stone unturned when trying to prepare the team, but it was just different and took some adjusting to. After this debacle I'd expected the scenario to be, 'Okay lads, we'll see you tomorrow at 2pm at the ground', the normal way of doing things. Not a bit of it. 'Normal time at the hotel then lads.' Groan from the lads. Of course no one told me I had just entered the film set for Clint Eastwood's *Heartbreak Ridge*, in which the troops had to constantly guess what was going on. I had to ask one of the chaps what it all meant.

Nearly all football managers are obsessed with preparation, or at least the ones I've met are, and maybe that is a reflection of the standard of team I played in. A good diet, lots of hard training, plenty of sleep, no alcohol and no late nights are expected. Many managers even endorse and encourage the virtues of early marriage in the belief that this will settle a player down and prevent indulgent behaviour. I was carrying out my life as far opposed to a manager's plan as one could get. I would say that 90 per cent of a footballer's performance is ability and 10 per cent preparation. A number of managers reverse this percentage. It is usually the bosses who have never played at the highest level who get all screwed up about preparation. They have often only played in the lower divisions, where they witnessed the huff and puff of a manager working with average talent and who is therefore trying to outmanoeuvre his opponent by superior preparation. He never witnessed a stalemate between Arsenal and Spurs broken by a moment of inspiration. All the stalemates he ever saw were broken by a mistake. The attitude to British team sports is to go for reliable players, but this is wrong. What are needed are inspirational players. Take, for example, the Arsenal players of that period. They had Ian Wright to bang in the chances created by Seaman's play-making; Bergkamp, who in one second destroyed hours of preparation with a moment of skill; and Paul Merson, who was class and lived a life on the edge. Here I was entering the world of endless, or, so they thought, meticulous preparation.

The norm for home games at Watford was to assemble at the Post House, just off Junction 5 on the MI, at 11.30am. Dinner or luncheon would then be served for 12pm by two Greek chefs and we'd all sit down together to have a good yarn. After the fodder, the lecture, *Monty Python* style, would begin. At around 12.45pm Harry would begin with some mention of the food being great and I'm sure he used to thank the Greeks for their service. I thought he was going to say grace before the food on more than one occasion. 'Right, the opposition. Well, me and Tom had a look at them mid-week. Didn't we, Tom?' 'That's right gaffer eh, we've got to get into 'em!' 'Yeah, they're a good side, you know, they knock it about well and they're solid. Don't concede much...' By the time he'd finished eulogising about them you would have thought the gaffer was their public relations officer. The next bit was to go through each member of their probable team, and he would always begin with me, talking about the right-back. 'Good pro, lots of experience, likes to get the ball to his feet and plays from there. Likes to get up and down the line, quite quick, puts a good ball in the box and can score if you let him *(most could score if you let them, Steve)*. Good defender and he's strong in the air. But get the ball and get past him!' said the Gaffer, without pausing for breath. It sounded like he should be playing for Brazil. 'Right,' I replied, somewhat stunned. The manager then proceeded to go through the rest of their team, painting very similar pictures. From here, at last, things returned to normal and we set off to the ground at 2pm. The hour before kick-off is supremely interesting and I shall deal with this at length shortly.

So there I was, about to make my debut against Everton. Imagine the scenario; I arrived at the hotel, fresh from Halifax, ready to face the best team in the land for the last three years, since they won the Championship in 1985. Everton were then denied their passage into Europe because of an evening's hooliganism. 'Do you know the full-back, Rick?' 'Er, well, I've seen him on the telly!' 'Gary Stevens – good pro, good pro, (all football coaches and managers repeat their sentences when coaching) good engine, gets up and down, blah, blah, blah.' In a nutshell he was saying, 'You're up against the best right-back in the country, doubled up with the best right-winger in the country (Trevor Steven)' and the technical advice is 'get the ball and take them on'. Brilliant. I know Harry was trying his best for me, attempting to ease me in, and he genuinely wanted me to do well. It was just funny the way he said things.

The game was played at one hell of a pace and, to make matters worse, Everton seemed to be playing everything down their right flank, obviously testing the rookie. After 10 minutes I was breathing though my arse. Suddenly I got the ball, the moment we'd all been waiting for. I mis-controlled it through Stevens's legs (an accidental nutmeg), went to cross it and slammed it up the rear of Steven. The resultant cannon propelled the ball towards the touchline and, as I went to retrieve it, I ran into Stevens and knocked him over. The ref stopped the game so both lads could receive treatment. I had made my mark.

'Go on and make something happen.' That was what I was told by my first-ever manager, Rod Turner, at Embsay Rovers, when he threw me on as a 13-year-old for the first team. I always tried to achieve that, no matter what. I didn't have too much impact on the game, but I certainly had an impact on the collective right flank of Steven and Stevens. Needless to say, we lost the game and ended up being relegated from the old First Division, even though Watford's best performances came during the last 10 games, including a 1–0 victory over Arsenal at Highbury, courtesy of a late winner from yours truly. Still, it was a great thrill to be involved at this level and I have Harry and Tom to thank for my chance.

After the relegation debacle, the following season was full of promise. Steve Harrison had made many useful pre-season signings to buoy up the squad and we were all in good spirits. We headed off to sunny Exeter in preparation for the season and set up a training camp at the university. Most other self-respecting clubs went to Norway, Sweden, Denmark or Finland, but no – we went to Devon. It was one of the funniest times of my pro career, as incident followed incident with amazing variation. We'd had our early morning Cooper's run around the dog track at Vicarage Road and then departed for Devon fully laidened up with butties. At Exeter Uni we were shown to our barracks and then reported for fodder at 1800 hours on the dot. The food was bog-standard student grub. We'd not heard of athletes' special-balanced diets. This was your mash spuds, mince and onions with half a loaf of bread to tackle it with. It was probably designed to soak up the alcohol that the management knew we'd partake of, and so it was a clever plan by Harry and Tom. The rooms had a sink (which doubled up as a toilet), a desk, a 1950s wooden wardrobe and an uncomfortable metal army camp bed. The following morning, on the way down to breakfast at 0700 hours, I passed Mel Reece's room and gave him a knock. He emerged, followed by a couple of cats, and by the end of the 10 days it resembled a cattery in his bedroom. We arrived at the playing fields a few miles out of Exeter, which had to be the largest unfenced strip of grass outside Yorkshire. There were no prizes for guessing what Tom was going to use it for – Kenny Jacket nearly had a heart attack.

After an hour of cross-country running around an area the size of half the Australian outback, we began to play some possession, again on a boundary-less area and topped off with some shuttle running. 'Where's the doggy boards, Tom?' said Harry. Doggy boards were one of Tom's inventions. They were solid Toblerone-shaped bits of furniture about two-foot long and a foot high which the lads did sprinting shuttles with. You ran between them, say 20 yards apart, and put your foot against them to get a quick turn in. Players dreaded them as Tom was obsessed by them and would makes us do loads of shuttle sprints until we couldn't stand up.

'Don'ts know gaffer, a packed 'em.' Truth was he had packed them. Tony Coton and I had flung them into a bloke's back garden down the lane next to the side of the ground prior to leaving. I never saw them again. Childish and irresponsible, I know.

About three or four nights into the tour, a few of us went out on the town following a practice game against Torquay United on the same expanse of grass, although luckily it had been marked out into something resembling a pitch. The evening was a disaster and landed us in serious hot water the following day. Neil Redfearn felt unwell in a taxi, obviously because of the way the cabbie was driving, and I got us all ejected from a local night club for dancing erotically to the Guns and Roses classic *Sweet Child of Mine*. Later on, in attempting to make off with an art student's artificial plastic head, which was drying on a third-floor window ledge, one of my colleagues fell off my shoulders and knocked his front two teeth out on the first-floor window sill. We made off with the head, got it back to HQ and hid the evidence under a bed. We came up with a pathetic excuse to explain why one of us now looked like Joe Jordan, with missing front teeth, and said that while getting up for a piss in the middle of the night, he'd slipped and stoved his teeth into the porcelain sink. Unfortunately some of the other chaps had invited themselves into a private party on the University grounds in a house owned by a German couple, and they had caused a riot by insulting their heritage and by inventing a new party game of sliding down the banister in the main hall – minus attire. They were subsequently ejected from the house with a volley of complaints. I still had the small matter of a very real-looking head to get rid of and, fearing that we would have to undergo the rigours of a door-to-door search, disposed of it down a drain a quarter of a mile away from the accommodation. God only knows what the man who discovered it when it blocked up the drain would have thought, as it was made of an endurable material and would not have rotted. The following morning we felt the backlash, and rightly so, from the boss who, following the warm-up, sat us all down and subjected us all to one of his fabled character assassination tirades.

'Player A, I bring you here from Blank United and how do you repay me? I'll tell you. You go out in pre-season, get pissed up, you nearly get us kicked off the campus by insulting the Germans in the bursar's house and then you stand under my window barking like a werewolf. How long have you had that f***in' cough anyway? You're a f***in' disgrace. You can go and get your stuff and f**k off back to London on the train. Tom, give him some money.' This was a fair assessment and perhaps deserved, but it would been better to have apologised to the Germans and fined him. Maybe he just wanted rid of him. Player A just stood up, said absolutely nothing and did exactly that. He cleared off. He was no stranger to controversy. I thought, 'Thank God he didn't know what I was up to last night,' and just as I was thinking that I'd escaped chastisement he suddenly rounded on me. 'Rick Holden. You've let yourself down associating with the likes of him. You should know better than getting pissed up and coming in late. Something happened last night, that's why Player B is at the dentist this morning. I bring you down here with nothing but a pot to piss in and what thanks do I get?' I can remember thinking, 'Any minute now I'll be joining him on Exeter station and that will be that.' I would go via the estate agent and put my newly bought, overpriced house on the market. But I didn't. Harry got distracted by another criminal and the verbal storm petered out. I thought that it was a little harsh and that all I had done was get a little high-spirited. Looking back, it was scandalous behaviour and one of the many traps you fall into as a young player.

The season went well and I played in most of it, helping us to stay top of the League with Chelsea and Manchester City, until round about March when the gaffer suddenly altered his tack. On Saturday 11 March we played Chelsea at Stamford Bridge and went into a quick-fire two-goal lead. This was soon squandered and I got some of the blame for my defensive abilities. Tony Dorigo had cut inside me at left-back – I was playing on the right wing on this particular day – and smashed an unstoppable 25-yarder past Tony Coton. My fault. I knew that the knives were out for me and the ensuing events of the season were no great surprise. I had worked out by now how the gaffer's mind worked and knew he would react like this. Things came to a head in our next away fixture at Bradford, on Saturday 18 March. Winning 1–0 with 15 minutes to go, I was substituted and replaced by Kenny Jacket. Kenny had recently won our in-house prize for Watford's stiffest man and used a combination of Ralgex heat rub, Wintergreen and WD40 in order to limber up. I admit, my body language wasn't the greatest at being dragged off, while the travelling band of followers who dared venture 'up north' gave me a rousing send off. I turned and applauded them in acknowledgement, but this was seen as undermining the manager's authority by the gaffer, and he grabbed hold of me and forced me down into the dug-out. I informed him that it was a mistake putting the equivalent of tin man on instead of me, which added further fuel to the fire. More angry words were exchanged and even a couple of handbag punches. He swung at me and hit Tom, and I returned the compliment and also copped Tom. To make matters worse, Bradford scored almost immediately after their right-back dispossessed my replacement and crossed the ball from the right flank. Two minutes later, to compound our misery, they scored again in a repeat of the first goal.

Foolishly, I pointed this out to Harry and he wasn't impressed with my observations. In the dressing room afterwards more than a few harsh words were exchanged and I can particularly remember lots of people having a few things to say. There was an icy air in the coach on the way home. After the delights that the Greeks served up, I was summoned to a meeting with the gaffer down at the front of the bus, where all managers sit. He told me how disappointed he was in me. My reaction was to inform him how disappointed I was in him. This stumped him, and we hardly ever talked again. I regret it now and know it was stupid. But when you're passionate, as both myself and Steve are, things get out of hand occasionally. The season petered out for Watford and perhaps we deserved to get nothing from it, the way we all behaved. The gaffer couldn't see that the disappointment shown was because I cared passionately about the club and the match we were involved in. Instead, he took it as a personal rap because he didn't really understand me. Yes, he was going to carry the cup of success and he was going to carry the can of shit if we failed. He would blame the players for failure, but we were all in it together and he knew that. It wasn't Harry's fault, we were all to blame, but I look back now in regret at not being mature enough to handle certain aspects of footballing reality. Football is, by its very nature, balancing on a razor's edge and is a ruthless business.

I played out the rest of the season in the reserves, and we lost on one occasion to Crystal Palace Stiffs (reserves) 6–0. Ray Graydon was in charge, and the following day he invited us all back to the club to explain ourselves. When it got to my turn for a self-condemning soliloquy, I stunned the audience, including the gaffer, by declaring that I thought I'd played well. This, needless to say, went down like a lead balloon and displays to you all what sort of character you were dealing with at that time. I had a good summer, however, playing cricket back in Yorkshire, and returned to the club full of optimism and drive. Although I was invited on yet another pre-season tour of Devon, it was fairly obvious that Glynn Hodges was going to be preferred on the left to me. This was a shame – at the beginning of the previous season Glynn had played on the right and I'd been on the left, and it worked a treat as we'd made a great start to the campaign, going straight to the top of the League! The balance of the side seemed good and then for some reason the gaffer changed it.

The end was a classic. We were due to play a friendly at Welling or some such place and were told to wear our red polo shirts to turn up to the game in. At the ground Harrison named the side and the subs and I wasn't among them. No explanation was forthcoming, so I just cleared off as soon as the game kicked off and waited until Monday morning. This was the final week before the season started, and I knew I had to act quickly in order to prevent a miserable start to my year. I knocked on the gaffer's door at the training ground at Stanmore and Harry took me into a side room to hear what I had to say. At first he started bollocking me about my attitude and qualified it with the example of me wearing the wrong polo shirt at the game on Saturday. Apparently I was wearing last year's version, which was a slightly different shade of red, and I'd let the side down. He must have thought that I'd done it deliberately to wind him up, but nothing was further from the truth. Quite simply, I had not yet grown out of my student approach to dress, which goes against the grain with professional footballers, whom as I have already pointed out tend to get a bit obsessed with clothes. I assured him it wasn't deliberate and then presented him with an envelope containing a request for leave, permanently. He handed it back to me and told me to save my money. I was to go home and wait for a phone call from Joe Royle, the manager of Oldham, that afternoon.

This was quite a turn around from a man with whom I'd had to haggle for my loyalty bonus several months earlier – he would have denied it ever existed if I hadn't kept a scratty bit of paper he scrawled it on. Now, quite generously, he was saving me the rest of my paltry signing-on fee, which players are generally expected to sacrifice if they request an early transfer. Maybe he felt sorry for me. After all, I still didn't have a pot to piss in. I had been conned into buying a house at well over the odds at £97,000 for a poxy semi-detached in Adeyfield in Hemel Hempstead, and I watched with incredulity as house prices slumped following the stock market crash of 1987. Not only that, interest rates went through the roof and my monthly mortgage payment blew through the £1,000 mark. I hadn't been diddled when I signed for the club at a cost of £125,000, as I had been given £10,000 signing on fee (which is not the usual 10 per cent), my loyalty bonus and the Elton John albums. But it was a minefield out there for an inexperienced lad. For years clubs have been bossing players and always held the upper hand, but now, if you are a good-quality player, the boot is on the other foot and the clubs don't like it. There could also be another sinister reason for my sale. When Halifax and Watford agreed the initial fee, there was an additional £25,000 payable to Halifax on me playing 50 League games for the club. Call it my deceitful mind, but they sold me on to Oldham on 42 League appearances. It was a surprise, therefore, when Steve Harrison refused my transfer request and saved me £3,333 in signing-on fees.

There it was then, a short and yet eventful trip down south over and done with. I had a great laugh at times and met some good people. I did actually learn a great deal about the game at Watford. It's just a pity it didn't last a bit longer, as I'm sure we'd have been promoted to the big time far quicker the club managed it in 1999. Still, I didn't bear any grudge against Steve, or anyone else for that matter; we footballers put it down to being all part of the game. Steve Harrison is a good bloke, who, if anything, got too choked up in trying to bring success to the club. He has since admitted verbally that he was too impatient with the northern boys he signed, like Lee Richardson and Neil Redfearn, and should have given us all more time to settle in. He was from the North himself and had lumped the ball into the Channel a few thousand times for Blackpool. I have taken in a lot of what he said and have used a great many of his coaching methods, apart from finishing in front of goal. I also learned a great deal about psychology and how not to indulge in amateur personality analyses. I think it's best to try to get the best out of people without resorting to character assassination. Perhaps it's best to accept that people are different and to try to live with those differences without attempting to change them into something they are not. That way, you'll have very strong characters all pulling towards the same goal and they will be able to share the burden of success and failure together. I returned home and told Jean that my time at Watford was at an end and her reply, as quick as a flash, was, 'Sign for anyone but Oldham.' This ridiculous bias was steeped in the fact that she was from the town full of chimneys originally and it had obviously left an indelible stain on her psyche. 'It's funny you should mention that,' I replied, 'because I'm expecting a call from Big Joe Royle any minute'. The silence was all-pervading.

The following morning I got the estate agent in to value the house, which I knew I shouldn't have bought but was pressured in to as it was the Watford policy. Some clubs used to insist that you purchased a dwelling within a certain radius of the club to show a sense of commitment and so it was easy to travel in and out of the place for training and games. Realising my mistake long before my departure, I've advised everyone I ever met in football not to buy a house on the edge of the city you happen to play for but back home, where you think you would like to live when you retire. This way you can travel around quite freely without the burden of a house hanging around your neck like a millstone, and you can always rent out your home until you require it. As I expected, I'd lost money. It was only worth £84,000, and I was skint. I told my dad of my predicament and he lent me a few quid, and Oldham, or more precisely Joe, promised to make up the difference when I eventually sold it. It's a good job that I made an impact on the scene because I didn't off-load it for nine months, and the club gladly made up the negative equity. I shot off up the motorway like a bat out of hell in my new express X-R3i. It was the price I paid for living too close to Essex. Jean had got a job in Hemel and decided to stay on to sell the house, and I would see her at weekends. We also had Mingan to think of – he'd been a real success down south and enjoyed himself very much. He spent his day basking in the sun after having got stoned out of his mind on catnip. By Thursday I had signed for Oldham and had been re-instated as a northerner by Saturday afternoon in my debut at Ewood Park.

Let's end with an amusing little anecdote at Watford. One weekend when Jean was away, a few of the players and I went out on the town after the game. We ended up at a night club in Hemel called the Living Room, which was renowned as a 'grab a granny' venue. Somehow, we'd been split up into two pairs. Myself and Lee Richardson, whose never-to-be-forgotten domestic skills included cleaning vomit up with the vacuum cleaner, and Tony Coton and Mel Rees, two daft 'keepers. Lee and I went for a curry, and the two rocket scientists went back to my house to wait for us to return. When we returned I found a cat-sized hole in the ceiling of my conservatory and Mingan sitting next to half a dozen empty lager cans. I was convinced for months that Mingan was the culprit; being a Leeds cat he would have no problem getting stuck into the drink. It hadn't really occurred to me that the two stooges had got bored of waiting for me to return and had broken in through my bedroom window, putting their feet through the roof as they climbed. That's goalkeepers for you. I cleared away the lager cans and, to this day, Jean thinks the hole was made by the cat jumping off the window ledge onto the conservatory roof.

I left Watford on a downer, never realising my full potential. It was sad to be leaving so many new and good friends behind, and I had built up a good rapport with the fans. What's more, I was leaving behind the makings of a very good side, and it was a shame to see it go down the pan in the next couple of years. Still, what did I care now? I had moved on.

# four

## Escape to Victory

I arrived to sign on at Oldham on the Thursday before the season was due to start. The place had an altogether different feel to it. It was much more homely and warm and yet seemed very professional at the same time. They seemed either very used to making new players feel welcome, or else it was purely natural. I was introduced to my new gaffer, Joe Royle, and his assistant, Willie Donachie, and then to the tea ladies, the cleaning ladies, the office staff and to just about everyone in the square mile I had just driven into. To be honest, I wasn't all that certain where Oldham actually was. For me it was just another damp northern relic of the Industrial Revolution stuck in a poverty trap as thick as the Lancastrian dialect. I'd played there the season before for Watford, but hadn't taken all that much notice of the location in exact geographical terms. This was unusual for me as I'm an avid map studier, and wherever I go I always buy a local chart of the area.

I had driven over from my dad's place at Skipton via Halifax, as I thought that this was the shortest route down the Pennines from the Dales to north Manchester. As Oldham is in fact 30 miles due south of Skipton, it poses a few problems with travel unless you've got a light aircraft, and there is absolutely no point in attempting to get there by train. The journey took longer than I anticipated and yet didn't seem that long as I had my sister Jen with me for company. It didn't interfere with her job as she's never had one (she has now but it took her a while). I brought her along as a contract minder, bearing in mind my experiences at Watford. I needn't have worried though as Joe looked after me very well and definitely was never one to screw a player out of his worth. After the formal signings we returned home via the Lancastrian roads, which is exactly the same mileage as the Yorkshire route, 48 miles, yet only takes 50 minutes if you know the odd moorland short-cut. Most of it is motorway until you reach Colne, and then you need to get your Ordnance Survey map out to avoid the wagon-jammed A58 to Yorkshire.

By Friday I was training with the squad in preparation for our opening fixture against Blackburn at Ewood Park. Training was radically different: a warm-up, a circle (piggy-in-the-middle), some crossing and shooting and then a cup of tea and home for lunch time. At Watford I often felt that I'd left much of my energy on the training pitch when it came to Saturday afternoon, but Willie's training suited me down to the ground. We lost to a bizarre opening goal when our goalie, Andy Rhodes, a fully paid-up member of the "keepers' union' (for which the main entry requirement is being crazy to the point of being certifiable) kicked the ball up the arse of the advancing striker, causing it to be returned straight into the back of the net. This was a feat he was to repeat in a Wembley Cup Final at the end of the season. I quickly realised that we were on to something special here at Oldham, though. Somehow, Joe had gathered a strange but gifted bunch of individuals and all we had to do was gel together as a team, then nothing would stop us. The gaffer and his staff must have had a rare talent for spotting reject players who were going nowhere or, at best, sideways to and from various clubs up and down the land, people who were not the easiest to handle but who were nonetheless very good once liberated from the constraints of regimented austere professional life and given belief and direction. What I'm trying to say is that, to many, these players were nobodies, seen as failures who were going to drift through the game without achieving much more than the odd headline for a drink-driving offence. Joe Royle took the player and gave him a second chance at Oldham. It was the ideal club for this philosophy to take root as expectations were low. The club seemed quite comfortable to remain in the Second Division and therefore gave the players the perfect incentive to perform well in the shop window. In other words: 'Do well at

Oldham and you'll do well anywhere.' We were, after all, as Joe himself said, all there because there was something wrong with us – a bit harsh,but true. After a week I knew that, although we were undoubtedly a collection of odd-balls, great things were around the corner as the talent became more and more apparent. Something was happening which was bringing all these players to the peak of their careers at the same time, though quite what that was is the most difficult thing to put your finger on. On a personal note I was happy again, as I was at a club very similar in nature to Halifax; a happy club without any airs and graces and run along the lines that I thought a professional football club should be run. I didn't have to wash my own blasted training kit, which was the case at Watford, and I didn't have to drive endless miles between the training ground and the club, wasting time and petrol, in order to attend a meaningless meeting. Things which could have been said in two minutes on the training field are, in many clubs, drawn out as everyone has to cross the town or city to go back to the club for a two-minute meeting. Small things do matter, and attention to detail is very important when running a successful soccer club, but attention to detail for the right reasons and not as an act of amateur psychology to try to keep the players on their toes or to deliberately piss them off. I often felt that at Watford things were done in order to remind me that I was lucky to be a footballer. I should, therefore, be grateful that I was playing for Watford and not doing a paper round up the side of Ben Nevis, delivering food hampers to the Scottish yetis or stuck down the pit in Barnsley up to my eyeballs in shit. I know they are right in that you are lucky to be a professional footballer, but did we always need reminding?

For the first game away to Blackburn Rovers, Joe came up to me after training and said, 'How are you getting to Blackburn?' I thought, 'Don't they have a team bus?' I assumed I'd go with them. 'I mean,' explained Joe, 'do you want to make your own way to the ground, as Skipton is closer to Blackburn than Oldham, to give yourself more time and rest.' I nearly fell over with the logic. What was this? I remembered the Glynn Hodges and Mark Morris experience when we played Crystal Palace. They were forced by Harrison to drive to Watford from Sutton (next door to Palace) to board the team bus and make the journey to the ground that way.

After the game they had to come back on the bus and then drive back home. I decided to get myself to Blackburn, but what about a pre-match meal and a team meeting? 'No, it's a waste of time. Just be there for 2pm.' I thought about this for a minute and then it occurred to me – where would I park the car? Was there a players' car park like at Oldham? 'Go and see Terry Cale, he'll look after you.'

Terry had joined the club on the same day that I had, but I thought by his relaxed manner that he'd been there forever. He was a smashing bloke and always looked after me like no other club secretary I've ever met before or since. Because of his mannerisms, he became known as Les Dawson and 'Les' was an absolutely different class. I went to see him, presented my dilemma, and two minutes later he returned with a pass for the directors' car park. That felt brilliant. This was a continuing feature for the rest of my time at Oldham, and I became the chief ticket-organiser for car parks away from home, with the help of Terry.

We did not start the season too convincingly, with the loss to Blackburn Rovers followed by a draw at home to Watford, a game in which I scored and had one disallowed by a linesman. It would not have been disallowed in today's interpretation of the rule of interfering with play. Quite amazingly, I refrained from running over to the Watford bench to exercise my right to freedom of speech. I thought that perhaps the goal was punishment enough and I knew that the writing was on the wall for my former boss. Player A wasn't quite so forgiving when he bumped into Harrison the next time. After being sent home in disgrace from the Watford pre-season tour of Exeter the season before, he was sold to a southern club whom we played at the end of the season. It was at the time of my exile from the team, but for some reason I was made to travel with the squad, probably because the reserves didn't have a game on the Saturday, so I witnessed the event at close quarters. The ball had broken free on the halfway line after Rod Thomas had been tackled and Player A came menacingly into the frame. He had ample time to compose himself and secure possession for his new team. Instead, he caught a glimpse of his tormentor from that dark day in Exeter sitting in the dug-out some seven yards away. Seemingly without hesitation, he let fly with a ferocious shot at the dug-out, with a result that I can best describe as similar to a golf ball pinging around a china and marble antique shop. More than a little stunned, and with a fair loss of dignity, Harry tried to protest at the outrage, and who wouldn't, but everyone else concerned with the event was too consumed with laughter to do anything about it.

Following the Watford game we fought out a 2–2 draw at home against Ossie Ardiles's team, Swindon, and then went up to play Newcastle United, who by now were minus Paul Gascoigne and had just been relegated to the Second Division. They were not a good side and yet we somehow contrived to lose the game. There was some scant consolation for me in that I scored my second goal in a week and one of the best I ever netted, which was an overhead bicycle kick from the edge of the box into the top right-hand corner. You could have heard a pin drop inside St James' Park. As we returned to Oldham, Joe collared me as we got off the team bus and said words to the effect, 'Don't worry, we're better than this. Just be patient.' This was great because he knew how much I wanted to make this thing a success, he must have been able to sense it.

Sometimes in the past, and I suppose to a certain extent now, my throwaway remarks have portrayed a sense of lack of commitment to a cause, when all I'm probably trying to do is defuse the situation and take the tension out. It was important for it to work at Oldham, as deep down my Watford experience had left me with a feeling of failure, and I didn't like that one bit. Yes, I could blame Steve Harrison and Tom and the ghosts of the past era of Graham Taylor, but in the end it was all down to me. And I was the one left with the memories, no one else, so I had to exorcise this from my psychological depths. In truth we had not made a good start and had to wait another week to put it right. When you lose a game it takes ages for next week to come round, and it's great if you've got a midweek match because you have the chance to quickly repair any damage and to put a few things back together. What made it worse for me was that back home in Skipton I was bumping into old mates, whether at the petrol station or – you've guessed it – in the pub, and they all had the same thing to say. After the initial pleasantries they would retort with, 'So Oldham – a bit of a backward step then from Watford eh?' This annoyed the hell out of me because these thick northerners, entrenched in the doctrine of grim Pennine town, were nothing compared to the glamour of a Hertfordshire Home Counties' club on the edge of London. 'So things didn't work out for you at Watford then?' translated as 'You've found your limit then and it's great to have the chance to pull you down.' I just used to say, 'Think of it as a sideways step,' but it still got to me.

It's a funny thing but people will try to pull you down, and since I moved to the Island I've discovered a really good analogy for this. It's called the 'Manx crab'. People here use this saying to describe an attempt to make it from the Isle of Man. Imagine a bucket of crabs on the quayside. The bucket represents the island and the crabs are the people. Suddenly one crab starts to climb up the side of the bucket and it looks for all the world that he's going to escape to victory. He looks down and sees the other crabs reaching out to him. It looks as though they want to join him. So he reaches down to give the nearest one a lift, and they drag him back down into the bucket again. This was how it was in Skipton. There was a lot of jealousy around the town when I 'made it' because many people thought other boys in the town had more talent than me, and because I came from a middle-class background in a twee village and went to the elitist Skipton Grammar School. My contemporaries were from a more traditional working-class environment and their failure and my success was attributed to me having more chances than them, and that's the biggest load of bollocks I've ever heard! Hence I was desperate to do well, and it was going to start on Saturday against Plymouth at home. This was our second fixture at Boundary Park on a Saturday afternoon, and we were going to make it count. Saturday 9 September also happened to be my 25th birthday, and it was the right time to explode on to the scene. We duly won, but only just, by three goals to two, and I scored again, which made it three in as many games. Something was happening. We clearly had to improve our defence as a team, but we were starting to gel. From this day we never looked back, and the next three years were a roller-coaster ride of great games with incidents on and off the field. These were the best three years of my life and it will be a pleasure to reminisce.

What was the reason for this outstanding success at what was basically an underachieving, unfashionable northern football club? Like many things it was multifactorial, but the first thing I want to concentrate on is the plastic phenomenon. In 1970–71 Oldham gained promotion from the Fourth Division by finishing third in the League. After three seasons of consolidation, Jimmy Frizzell led them into the Second Division as champions of the 1973–74 campaign. This was a great thing and was greeted with wild celebrations in this virtual soccer wilderness. From that time until 1991 the Latics remained in Division Two, a period of 17 full seasons. That consistency at this level says something, but it looked as if Oldham had plateaued, and I suppose anyone who studies such things was waiting for either the nightmare season or the miracle season. In 1986 Oldham took a gamble and joined the plastic gang, which included QPR, Preston and Luton, by ripping up the grass pitch and replacing it with an artificial astroturf surface which we referred to as the 'plastic paradise'. This made perfect sense at Oldham because it has got to be one of the coldest, wettest, windiest and most inhospitable places to play football anywhere in the world. I noticed this when I first signed as there were yetis in the crowd wearing overcoats and even Geordies used to wear a vest under their T-shirts when they visited us. Not without reason was Boundary Park named 'Ice Station Zebra' by Joe. This new pitch meant that we wouldn't see games called off due to a water-logged pitch, but it made little difference if it snowed, because when it snows in Oldham you can forget it. The four plastic pitches in England were all different in the amount of 'bounce' in the surface. Luton's was a high bounce and QPR's was ridiculous. I can't really comment on Preston's because I never played on it, but those who did said it wasn't as bad as the two southern teams, but not as good as Oldham's. Our pitch had a low bounce and was good under foot in that you could grip very well if you had the correct footwear. All-weather pitches need attention and one of the most amazing things I ever saw was the groundsman watering it. Without this the pitch would dry up and crack. The composition is very fine artificial blades of grass (fibrillated polypropylene) with millions of sand and salt grains intermingled, a layer of 23mm to be precise. The pitch sits on top of a dense layer of rubber, although it was probably concrete at QPR, underneath which was 65mm of macadam and 225mm of crushed and graded stone. It was a fairly complicated process to lay.

There is a particular way of playing on plastic and it is not dominated by the short game as many people seem to think. I used to watch the prey training on the pitch on Friday afternoons in preparation for the next day's run around and I knew we would win if they started playing five-a-side tippy-tap football as their main approach. I remember the look of horror on Tony Adams's face when, after five minutes of Arsenal possession, we won the ball and crashed it over his head for a straight-running race against Ian Marshall. What was going through his mind as he ran towards his own goal with an ogre bearing down on him on skiddy plastic? We used to say that defenders looked like dogs on lino on the plastic paradise, and certainly if you got wrong-footed at pace it could have drastic consequences. Every opposing manager who visited and got stuffed used to have a little moan about the surface and very often intimated that it gave us an unfair advantage. To be fair, Graham Taylor didn't moan, he just praised us. It was more their approach that turned Saturday afternoons into a 90-minute crossing and shooting training session, not the pitch. The pitch was certainly tailor-made for me because I wasn't exactly a speed merchant, yet I could turn quickly and create good angles. I very quickly learnt to utilise my main ability, which was the early delivered cross. The low skidder behind the back four between the goalie and the six-yard box was deadly, and if Roger Palmer or Andy Ritchie or whoever didn't score, then a defender probably would. Playing on this surface gave me extra confidence to hit the moving ball as it was a 'bobble'-free pitch. The bobble is one of the most irritating things in the game. Through no fault of your own a bobble can reduce the greatest of players to a quivering nervous wreck and produce horrendous moments of embarrassment in front of thousands or even millions of fans. In case you don't have a clue what I'm talking about, a bobble is a freak bounce just at the moment of impact, causing the striker or defender to totally miss-cue the ball, usually behind the goal if you are a winger. The more uneven a surface is, the more likely you are to get a bobble, whether from the pitch being too dry and rutted or too wet and full of divots. In the old days, which is anything pre-dating 1990, you'd get winter bobbles and summer bobbles, and the best time of the year would be August and September. After this the pitches would cut up and we'd be into bobble season.

Even if the groundsman had tried to roll the pitch, by half-time there would be fresh bobbles everywhere. Towards the end of the season the playing surface would be rock hard and tiny bobbles would appear everywhere. Nowadays pitch technology has advanced so much that you very rarely get anything less than a bowling green to play on. Football pitches are so good that you'd settle for them in your front room as a carpet. If you can cast your mind back to the 1970s or if you ever get chance to see footage of an old game on TV, you will see huge, black, diamond-shaped patches of mud in the middle of the pitch. The only grass would be near each corner flag, and even Wembley suffered. You should see the 1970 FA Cup Final between Leeds and Chelsea, what a mud bath that was. They used to have the Horse of the Year show on it – how daft can you get?

We had no such problems at Oldham and, if anything, it worked against us as we'd have to readjust back on to bobbly grass when we played away. Complaints were voiced about the hardness of the surface, both on the body during running and jumping and if you were unfortunate enough to bite the dust. At the moment there is a lot of controversy over the deliberate dive and the conning of referees by forwards in order to win penalties or free-kicks in dangerous places. You would soon eradicate this if you brought back plastic. No one in their right mind would deliberately fall on this stuff. Rather worryingly, a few back complaints have emerged from players of this particular era, myself included, but it would be very difficult to prove that it was as a result of playing on this surface. Knowing what I do about biomechanics, it is sufficient to say that the forces would be increased through the various joints which take impact, like the ankle and knee, than would be the case on grass. Certainly the vanquished opposition would often leave Oldham with a parting shot along these lines; however, the plastic often just exposed their lack of technique and tactical nous, and the criticism was mainly sour grapes.

One problem which has still not been overcome on artificial surfaces is that of friction burns, and any kind of fall (deliberate or not) on Boundary Park left you with a burn of some description. When one thinks of friction injuries, it produces a picture of sliding  several feet along a surface; however, on our pitch if you just dropped to earth vertically without any horizontal motion, you would still more than likely end up with a do-it-yourself skin graft. When you did remove some skin at high velocity, it reminded you of your school playground days when you fell on the unforgiving tarmac, but to make it worse you literally had salt rubbed into the wound due to the composition of the pitch. Treatment of these injuries was difficult as they were no good dressed. Unless they were particularly deep and large in surface area they were best left to dry out, but you couldn't just sit in the changing room for three hours and wait for this to occur. You had to get dressed and go and meet people, whether it was the press or sponsors or family and friends. Several hours later and a cry would be let out as, during a sudden movement, you ripped some of the newly formed scab off the wound as it had stuck to the inner lining of your trousers. I was always doing this and recently, while digging through my old suits, I noticed patches of exudate on the lining of my trousers around the hip region, usually on the pocket. This was the classic when you thrust your hand into your pocket to buy a round (although some I won't mention rarely did this) and you wrenched your pocket off from the side of your leg and, rather pathetically, it hurt. At night, when awoken by the urge to have a pee, you might find that you'd taken the bed sheets with you and left your partner uncovered in the cold, or you might stand on the sheet and rip it from your leg. The worst, however, was when a newly formed Saturday scab was ripped back off on a Tuesday night, and that did bring tears to your eyes. Getting hot water on it from the shower and bath was no fun either. One of the best and most comical burns on the plastic was sustained by Frank Bunn who, in rapid pursuit of a flick on from Andy Ritchie, tripped and fell headlong into the spiteful turf, sustaining a beautiful graze on his more-than-prominent chin. What was particularly amusing was that, apart from the fact that it lasted for months, they had to replace the patch of astro that Bunny's chin assaulted. We had a phrase, probably introduced by Joe, which he reminded his defenders of when faced with a tricky opponent: 'Introduce him to the plastic.' The result was often to concentrate the player's mind for a while after the incident. The fear of falling on this stuff can never be understated and may have been one of the reasons for many a team's tentative approach at Boundary Park.

Another factor which has to be given some attention is the weather, which in Oldham's dour Pennine district is pretty grim. This had a profound effect on the local population, let alone the visitors. There's a picture of Billy Spurdle in August 1957 leading the troops out at Boundary Park and, though himself in short sleeves, he is being watched by a crowd who are dressed for the Antarctic in their top coats, scarves and flat hats. This gives you some impression of what the weather was like. To say it got cold is an understatement and, with the wind whistling off Saddleworth Moor, the wind-chill effect caused the temperature to drop to freezing and below. You eventually got used to it, and it certainly helped our pass and move game as it was not wise to stand still for too long in those conditions. The opposition, particularly southern opposition, did not take too kindly to playing footy on Tuesday nights in a refrigerator and used to dress accordingly. A game against Ipswich Town is apocryphal in that they ran out in gloves and tights and then were dispatched in the snow 4–0 without mounting a single attack on the Latics' goal. They may as well have mailed Oldham the points and saved money on the travel expenses.

The single most important fact, however, overlooked by many, is that it was a bloody good team assembled for next to nothing on a shoestring budget, and for this Joe Royle must take the accolades. He had the ability to find talent that was going nowhere, but who were hungry for success in that they needed to prove themselves, and also, as in my case, were skint. He threw this bunch of nomads together and suddenly it took off. Joe called me the catalyst, the final piece in the jigsaw, or more correctly the final loony in the mad house, and yet in my opinion he was still wrestling to find his best starting line-up. This didn't materialise until 28 October against Wolves at Molineux, although there really wasn't anything to choose between the goalkeepers. Rhodes was in goal behind full-backs Barlow and Irwin and centre-halves Barrett and Warhurst. In midfield there was Henry and Milligan, with wingers myself and Adams, and up front Ritchie and Bunn. Hallworth (the 'captain') was to share the goalkeeping responsibilities, while Roger Palmer was to handle a great deal of the attacking duties, scoring as regularly as ever. Ian Marshall became a utility man able to fit in at centre-half but more and more carving out a striking role for himself when he got the opportunity. Gary Williams became an ever-present on the bench, and Willie Donachie's exceptional fitness allowed us to use him as cover once or twice when needed. Joe bolstered the squad later in the season with the addition of Scott McGarvey, once of Manchester United, Paul Moulden, formerly of Manchester City, and my ex-teammate, Neil Redfearn, from Watford.

Joe had a thing about goalkeepers and would quickly change personnel if he thought that one was having a bad time. Rhodes was fully paid up in terms of the 'barking mad school' and except for the odd bout of depression, which gets us all, was more or less consistently manic, which is ideal material for a goalie. Captain Hallworth was an altogether different kind of eccentric, not loud but more quirky, which meant he was more stable than a lot of 'keepers, although when he flapped he resembled a giant rooster running around trying to protect his chickens (defenders) from invading foxes (strikers). Jon made milk look flushed and his legs looked like they were on backwards when he ran. Andy Barlow was a 'Steady Eddie'. We did very well as a pair when I could get him into my way of thinking, and he was one of the few full-backs that I could get to pass me the ball on a consistent basis. Dennis Irwin was the other full-back, who went on to great things with Manchester United and Ireland. Mike Milligan and Nick Henry were christened 'yard dogs' by Joe and literally used to snap away at the heels of the opposition midfield with ceaseless energy. When these two won the ball they slid it to me and Neil Adams on the flanks and we supplied the ammunition for the big guns up front, and that is a basic description of how we used to play. Of course, there was a lot more to it than this, but needless to say it was a very simplistic and effective approach which, when on song, would destroy the best of organised teams.

We had a bad start in the 1989–90 season, drawing and losing too many games early on, and it appeared as if the side was trying to gain cohesion and confidence. This began to come to the fore as a result of the Cup runs in the League Cup and FA Cup. Putting sides like Arsenal, Everton, Aston Villa, West Ham, Southampton and Leeds to the sword, not just by riding our luck, but through totally dominating them, seemed to give everyone a lift which carried over to the following season.

Sadly we finished with absolutely nothing to show for our endeavours in 1990 and suffered the traumas of semi-final defeat in the FA Cup against Manchester Utd after a replay and losing to Nottingham Forest 1–0 at Wembley in the League Cup Final, a disastrous end to a competition we had totally dominated. In the League we finished outside the Play-offs in eighth position and to this day I can remember the empty feeling as I drove back home to Skipton after our last game at Bradford. We had an open-top bus ride around the town after the League Cup Final and, although it was a lovely gesture from the town to the players and fans, I did not want to be there and couldn't wait for the next season to begin. Why had we ended up empty-handed? Fatigue had undoubtedly had something to do with it, as between 19 August and 7 May, a period of roughly 38 weeks, we played 65 games. This works out at a game every four days, and with a small squad of players this will take its toll. I had played in 64 and couldn't raise a gallop at the end. I felt that I hadn't done myself justice and this would have to be put right next season. I had one excuse in that towards the end of the season I had to play every game with a painkilling injection in the bottom of my foot to relieve a condition called Morton's neuroma. This is the pinching of nerves in the tarsal tunnel, which feed the toes. When my foot made contact with the ground, the nerve was compressed and I received an electric shock in the end of my middle toe, which was disconcerting and sometimes quite painful. The painkilling injections worked after about 20 minutes and lasted until about an hour after the game had finished. We did try to get to the bottom of the problem and the finest minds in the North West examined my left foot. While they were all unanimous in the opinion that my feet belonged to a gorilla, nobody could fix the problem. I had to give it some thought and came to the mind-numbing conclusion that my boots were too tight. This is was not because I'd laced them up with too much enthusiasm, but because the astro-turf boots that we'd all been given were too narrow at the medial arch of the foot and hence were pinching the joints of my toes on impact with the astro. The answer was simple, and it was left to me to find the solution. If I wore larger boots I'd have been running around like a pelican with flip-flops on as I was already in size 10 boots. I have very wide feet and possibly the ugliest in professional football in the

Fresh from winning the Schools' Cross-Country Championship in my first year at Ermysted's Grammar School. I got back before the officials.

Mingan the cat, who was well-travelled on the footy highway. The Leeds stray with attitude was in a minging condition when we found him in 1985. He retired by the sea in Peel in 1996.

Famous faces in the Halifax Town squad of 1986.

Frank Harrison and I do the Carnegie, Halifax's retro dance.

More Fourth Division clatter-bang action – look at the state of the pitch!

An early deception against lookalike permed Swansea City defenders in the game at Halifax Town. This match liberated us from the bottom of the Football League.

Mick Galloway went on to play for Celtic. Billy Bar looks on.

The Halifax squad of 1987. Famous faces include Phil Brown, Mick Matthews, Micky Galloway, Lee Richardson, Wayne Allison, Billy Ayre and Dave Longhurst.

I'm trusted with free-kicks at Halifax. Phil Brown and Mick Matthews observe.

**Launching myself into the air and probably getting a bollocking from Steve Harrison at the same time at Maine Road against City.**

**Me and Brian Talbot do a new dance.**

**Muddy confusion at Brighton in 1988.**

**Playing for Watford at Boundary Park in 1989. Neil Adams, who was to become my crossing partner-in-crime, peers over my shoulder looking like his nickname, 'Bert' out of *Sesame Street*.**

Doing what wingers should – compete with the forwards on crosses. A youthful Gary McAllister peers through my armpit.

An old First Division match against QPR. The wide arm swing was to bat off the defender.

**Outdoing a Newcastle defender in our epic fourth round Cup tie against the Geordies in 1989, which I killed with a ridiculous deflected shot off poor old Glenn Roeder.**

**Action from Vicarage Road in 1988–89.**

**More dancing at Watford in the old First Division.**

**The Three Amigos. Lee Richardson and Wayne Allison followed me to Watford and this picture was taken at The Shay in a pre-season friendly against Halifax. Note the skip in the background!**

**My debut in the big time for Watford against Everton in March 1988. Trevor Steven gives chase.**

**My first day of signing in 1989.**

My first game away to Blackburn Rovers.

Joe reminds me that we had better win this second replay versus Everton. He knew we had been out on the Thursday.

Liberation! Our first home goal in the top flight against Chelsea for 67 years, which I scored, in a 3–0 win.

Another attempted overhead kick at Newcastle.

**Putting Paul Parker under pressure at Wembley.**

**A long-range shot, which went into the top corner, versus Aston Villa in the 3–0 FA Cup quarter-final win.**

last 50 years, so the solution was to take a pair of size 10s and remove the inner soles to create more room. They also needed to be softer and more pliable, so instead of opting for the Tom Whalley approach (knocking hell out of the boots on a wooden bench), I used to spend many an hour in the bath with nothing on except my new footwear. This did do the trick, although even today if I'm not careful I can set the thing off, so I always rip the sole out of my new shoes, but I don't go as far as sitting in the bath with a new pair of brogues on. I decided, though, that I also wasn't fit enough and went away with this in mind, determined to do something about it.

That summer of 1990 a was different class and was one of my most memorable, and probably the only one that I truly enjoyed during my time as a professional footballer. I didn't have any responsibilities, being child-free, and could do most anything that I wanted. I had by now moved back home to my village of Embsay, as during the season I had lived above a glass shop in Springhead (in the northern foothills of Oldham) called Garforth Glass. This shop belonged to my wife's cousin's husband, Julian Garforth, and was previously lived in by Jean's Aunty Nellie, who unfortunately died of cancer this same year. He charged me a nominal fee of £50 a week, and although this did me a favour in that I could well have lived in more luxurious surroundings for a greater price, I was still skint and struggling to make ends meet. He was also not slow in coming forward for free tickets for all the big games, which I had no real problem with, but it just went to show the often false perception the general public has of the wealth of footballers.

The place I lived in at Embsay was an ancient stone cottage, with three-feet thick walls, on the same row as the Scissors Inn, the boozer frequented by Oliver Cromwell when on his jaunts through Yorkshire. The bloke next door was a nutter who lived with his equally eccentric mother, and they seemed to specialise in shouting and bawling at each other about who had wasted the family fortune. The problem was that she was deaf and he was often fried to the tonsils, which made for a right old combination, and the walls just weren't thick enough. During the summer I played lots of cricket to keep myself fit and was on a 'pint a wicket' contract, which drove me on to an average of five wickets per match, which was a great start to a Saturday night, but I gave most of them away as I was trying to get fit. Fast bowling did great things for my fitness and it stood me in good stead for pre-season training, although it could have contributed to my long-term back problems. I then made my annual pilgrimage to the Scottish island of Islay, a place of outstanding charm, beauty and eight whisky distilleries – an absolute paradise. I was joined by Melt and his girl, Alison, and by Brown and his father-in-law, Brian, the landlord of our favourite pub in Ripponden, the Fleece. We spent a week eating lobster, drinking malt whisky and talking bullshit, a thing we all excelled at. Then it was back to reality.

Pre-season was spent tramping around the hills of Saddleworth (no problems as I had been running up Embsay Crag all summer) and playing local teams like Wrexham, Bradford, Halifax Town and, oddly, Banik Ostrava to prepare us for the intensity of competition ahead. After the heroics of the previous season we were now household names, and the opposition wanted to prove themselves against us, none more so than Craig Fleming of Halifax. 'Norland', as he was eventually christened when he joined us a year later, proceeded to kick me up hill and down dale for 90 minutes like his life depended on it. It probably did, as he must have sensed he was being watched by Joe and obviously wanted to leave a big impression on us both. Norland was very strong and very quick and had been training with the first team since he was about 13. He was now 19 but looked 30. This was what the rugged Pennines did to a lad, and he was a living image of the millstone grit surroundings that he was dragged up in. Unfortunately, he didn't get picked up by a really big club after his spell at Oldham and yet would have done a great job as a stopper in any Premier League side. He was also the worst player of the card game Hearts I've ever seen, but they probably only played snap in his early days at the Shay.

We started the season like a house on fire with five consecutive wins, and everything in the garden was rosy. Then something happened that made me stop in my tracks and brought me down to earth. On 8 September we travelled to Barnsley, a place that we'd had mixed fortunes at in previous encounters and the only place I ever had course to lose my rag with Joe. The year before we had gone down 1–0 at Oakwell, and during the game a bizarre incident led to me almost getting sent off.

The ref went down with a calf strain and had to be replaced by one of the linesmen. He in turn had to be replaced, and the lad who came on looked like a dwarf version of Eddie 'The Eagle' Edwards. He was obviously a local wag well-known to the Barnsley faithful. By this I mean he refereed in the local Leagues, and he was cheered as he ran on to the pitch and returned the compliment with a fist-clenched wave. Two minutes later I played the ball off the full-back and the little dwarf signalled a throw-in to Barnsley, throwing his head back and thrusting his flag-waving arm across his body. I said, 'You're joking,' at which point the goblin started a frantic military flag-waving routine to draw the new referee's attention. I was in close proximity during the resultant exchange between the two brain surgeons and it went like this: 'Yes, what is it?' 'The number 11, sir, called me a f***in' cheating bastard, sir,' at which point the ref took out a yellow card and brandished it at me. This was strange behaviour to say the least and obviously made the lad's year, and you could just see him boasting down the pub that night holding court with his mates. Oddly enough, years later when I joined Barnsley as physio in 2004, this bloke was the first person I bumped into, and he remembered the incident with a glint in his eye. A weird place, Barnsley. The year before I was visiting with Watford, and as I stood waiting to take a corner I became aware of a sharp pain in the right buttock. I spun around and saw a crab apple on the deck, which was obviously the offending article. I looked at the policeman standing next to me and he just shrugged his shoulders as if to say, 'They're strange here, mate, don't worry about it.'

Back to the Halifax game. We were in a determined mood and just blanked out any background irritation from the home fans. We were out-played at times, but thankfully came away with a 1–0 win due to a goal from Ian Marshall. We took an unbelievable amount of fans to the game and they completely filled one end of the ground. Afterwards, we were understandably delighted but while celebrating in the dressing room news filtered through of a death at York. I ascended the steps to the portacabin, which was where the players' lounge was, and as Captain Hallworth passed me a drink I asked him if he knew who it was that had died. He said that he didn't recognise the name so I chipped in with, 'It won't have been "Longy". He's very fit!' But Hallworth confirmed that it was, in fact, Dave Longhurst, my old teammate at Halifax. I couldn't believe it. I sat in silence for 10 minutes thinking about him. I'd seen him recently at Phil Brown's wedding, and we'd spent all night reminiscing about Shay days.

I had been due to see him the following day at my birthday bash in Skipton when, for the first time in a long time, we would all get together. This had promised to be as great as the last time we met, in Ripponden in 1988, we had caused a major earthquake with our collective spirit, resulting in a ban from several drinking establishments after an incident involving toilet humour, an ashtray and a pool table. I drove back to Skipton pondering this insane news and I suppose that disbelief is the only way I can describe how we all felt at the time. This was a very fit bloke who seemed to have boundless energy and displayed this on and off the pitch, usually with great hilarity. Several of his quirky habits still bring a smile to me, such as his deliberate angled parking of his car in the Halifax Town car park when he arrived often with only seconds to spare for training. This would provoke a reaction from the management, who would leap into the dressing room and tell Longy to move his f***ing car. He would, but he would still leave it at an obtuse angle, only in a different place. This would provoke another reaction and so on and so forth. My favourite Dave Longhurst story, however, is the one involving underwear. Professional footy players have their underwear provided for them, both for training and playing, and they are called slips. They are made of white cotton fabric and are manufactured by Umbro and other such companies. For some reason, at Halifax they were always one pair short and often there were many with holes in them, which interfered with your tackle. The trick was to get to training early in order to grab a good pair. Longy, as I have mentioned, often cut it fine, resulting in him always being short of a slip. On one particular occasion he arrived during the warm-up and joined the fray to cheers and derisory comments about him being fined for being late. The man giving out the most stick was called Alan Knill, who is a very tall 'streak of pumpwater' sort of bloke from Southampton. Longy accelerated past him and dropped his shorts. There was a moment's pause while the impact of his action sunk in and then, resembling a Billy Connolly animal impression, the giraffe-like Knill gave chase. 'You bastard' and other such expletives were uttered as a little and large double act unfolded in front of us. Longy was not a tall lad but he was a thoroughbred when it came to the dash, and Knillsy soon gave up the gallop. By this time Longy, being now a good distance from the pack and with his shorts now completely removed, was in pole position to carry out his final act. The reason for the commotion was that he was wearing Knill's bright yellow underpants, and he ran and slid on his backside through a muddy pool of water which was behind the goal. Mud and bright yellow don't mix, and the undergarment was ruined. Still, it livened up the day no end, and the game was better for people like Dave Longhurst. His endearing personality burns brightly and you can go and sit in the Dave Longhurst stand at York City and ponder on how much better today's media-hyped, money-oriented game, run by clean-cut, sterile individuals, would be with more people like Longy. I miss Longy. Minging.

Life went on. We still had the party in Embsay and got wrecked in his memory, which resulted in my wife being highly embarrassed by the strip I performed in front of everyone at the front door of my cottage. The tragedy inspired me to knuckle down and to work hard in order to achieve success at Oldham, and it also taught me to relax on the field. This wasn't as much of a problem at the Latics with Willy and Joe at the helm as it had been at Watford. The Oldham approach was very laid back compared to Watford, which used to make me on edge, frightened of defeat and ultimately overly anxious during the game. A constant barrage from the side lines yelling at me to do this and do that from the collective even affected my touch on the ball, whereas at Boundary Park all you heard from the bench was the odd joke and accompanying laughter. I was still anxious for success, however, and this used to make me uptight and nervy before a game, but after Longy's death I was never again worried on the pitch. What did losing a game mean now if you'd given your all?

Early exits from the FA Cup and League Cup helped our cause and rumours about a deliberate demise were not true, although it greatly relieved the tension, allowing us to concentrate purely on securing a place in the big time. There was a lot of expectation and we didn't want to fail. The season raged on, interrupted by the weather and occasional defeat. After a run of 17 games without losing we suffered two consecutive reverses to Port Vale and Bristol Rovers, who at the time shared Bath's ground. I was injured for these two games, but such was the 'joie de vivre' in the camp that I tootled along and witnessed each game for myself. All I can really comment about concerning the anatomy of the defeats is that a mixture of downright misfortune and sheer bad finishing in front of goal contributed to the losses, but it did not dampen our spirits at all. We soon put it right in the following two home games back on the plastic, and looking back this mid-season blip was only to be expected and demonstrated the belief in the camp in that it didn't seem to affect the confidence of the lads. Confidence was high as a result of the previous season's exploits and schoolboy ignorance. What I mean by this is that when you're young you've not heard of psychology and never pondered on the meaning of defeat. Quite simply, when in the flush of youth, defeat is merely dismissed as a momentary kick in the balls and is quickly forgotten as the excitement of playing another game rushes across the soul. Psychology destroys athletes as much as it helps them, and while practical psychology exists in every walk of life, the academic study of it with footballers sometimes does not work. We had an approach which was something like a boarding-school mentality mixed with outright lunacy. Dressing-room banter has always been important, and whenever I could I did everything to promote and harness this factor. During this season Willie Donachie had the idea of feeding us after training on fruit, rather like they do at the zoo. This novelty was quickly stopped after the gaffer discovered we were having fruit fights in the dressing room after training. They were so excessive that the bath looked like a giant bowl of punch and the dressing floor resembled the banks of the Serengeti after feeding time. This is an appropriate description as we did have several wildebeests in the squad. The fruit supplement seemed to work, the idea being that early ingestion of carbohydrate from fruit helped to speed up the muscle glycogen levels (recovery) following a game and a hard training session. This, together with the fact that we were worked very hard, meant that we could wear teams down, out-run them and ultimately overpower them. An example of this was the game against Portsmouth at Fratton Park. From start to finish we dominated the game, crushing them 4–1, their consolation coming from a Martin Kuhl penalty after Neil Redfearn had brought him down with a lazy challenge, which was unusual as there was never anything lazy about Neil. The game was won at a canter, we never really got out of second gear, and we knew that if we could do this away from home then we wouldn't have too many problems on our travels.

It was on journeys such as this that the endless card schools kicked in. Hearts was played to oblivion by a few of us, while another altogether dafter school played Aces to Kings and Chase the Ace – highly intellectual of course! The forfeit in these games stung you in your pocket, whereas our penalties were 'mooning' at passing wagons. Things were going so well at the time that all Joe had to worry about on Monday morning was the telephone and the postman bringing him complaints about our off-the-field behaviour from our antics on a Saturday night. Many of his early mornings must have been spent working out the best way to address a complaint, but he mainly dealt with it up front out on the training pitch: 'Just two minutes of your time, lads, before we start. I've had a letter from a wagon driver who claims that one of you stuck two fingers up at him on the motorway on Saturday afternoon on the way to the game. Now who's responsible for this?' Lots of schoolboy sniggering ensued until someone owned up. 'He f***ing deserved it. He was giving me the same but he won't have mentioned that.' 'Well, just use your brains when dealing with the general public, we can do without bad publicity,' was the usual response from Joe. Imagine that. A big butch wagon driver writing in to complain about a 'V' sign. He probably received about a dozen of these every day on the road. But it seems that an element of the general public will go to any length to get a player in trouble. Take a look at the letter Joe found on his desk about me (see picture section after page 96). When I threatened legal action he backed down and said he must have been mistaken. I'm not saying we footballers are always innocent, and we are certainly not angels, but the manner in which the tell-tale brigade approach us could be a lot better.

This is a classic to give you an example. Willie Donachie's idea of fun during pre-season training was to run the lads into the ground on the moors above Oldham. Joe lived at a place called Badger's Edge and we trained under his watchful eye from his balcony. As it was the first time most of us had been there, we did the usual thing and got lost on the way. Being late is not an option for professional footballers and excuses are just dismissed no matter what may have happened. This used to prey on my mind so much that I used to always leave an hour earlier than I had to on the day of a game in case of 'rhinoceros on the motorway' or some other such excuse. Any footballer with half a brain will also have six different approaches to the ground or training pitch in case of incidents outside their control. Having got lost had made us late, so when we arrived we parked up where we had been told to by the gaffer in the car park of a small golf club. It didn't seem to be obtrusive as it was a massive area of gravel with only a few cars on it. We were only a few yards into our stride when a bloke appeared like Mr Benn and without so much as an 'excuse me' proceeded to inform me that we weren't allowed to park there. I inquired as to where it would be possible to leave my vehicle, to which he replied that he didn't know but that we still couldn't park there. There was only one thing for it. I told him to 'f**k off and get a life', and off we went to our torture. A couple of hours later we were doing some exercises in a remote gym in Oldham when Joe walked in. 'I've just had the steward of the golf club on the phone complaining about one of you lot this morning. Is it the even-money Marshy or the two-to-one odds-on favourite Rick?' More muffled squirming laughter could be heard as I owned up and defended myself against the accusation of being a foul-mouthed yobbo. Still, these off-the-field incidents didn't affect the team's performances and we stumbled onto the Championship title. We only had one minor hiccup at Oxford, where for some reason we all played like complete novices and were trounced 5–1. I was subbed during this game and as there was no room on the bench for me to sit down, I had to lie down on a low wall. This left an enduring image in the minds of my fellow players and they still reminisce about the debacle at Oxford United when I lay on the wall.

Promotion was achieved at Portman Road, where we overcame an obdurate . Ipswich Town with two goals by Ian Marshall. It was a 'life-altering event' and marked the beginnings of many a good career at the highest level. It proved to everyone that Oldham and its players were capable of attaining football in the top

League. Whether we were good enough to survive was another matter, and there was only one way to find out – get there on merit. Having got there, we needed to win the Championship, as we had been top or in second place all season. West Ham were above us and they faced Notts County at home, who had been a thorn in everyone's sides all year. We always seemed to suffer at their hands and Neil Warnock's side was on a roll. I was confident that they would defeat the Hammers; they needed to in order to win a place in the Play-offs. Could we overcome Sheffield Wednesday, however, who had been up with us all season and had secured their return to the top flight? They were led by Ron Atkinson and were no mean team. I've only met Ron on a couple of occasions and he seemed great fun, and his record as a manager was excellent. I always thought he was good value when commentating on TV and he made some great points until he blew it.

We had played Sheffield in a cracking game down at Hillsborough in front of 34,000 and blown a two-goal lead by conceding two late penalties. This time it was Wednesday who took a two-goal lead as they battered us for the first hour. Then came our first bit of real fortune in two years, and it made up for the Cup Final and semi-final defeats of the previous campaign. Until now I was beginning to believe that one of the lads had been walking under ladders and another was running over black cats on the way to work. At 2–0 down I began to fear the worst, until a series of deflections set up Ian Marshall for a goal and then another deflected shot from Paul Bernard brought us level. With a few minutes remaining I skin-grafted myself in winning the ball back and it found its way to Andy Barlow who, under pressure from John Sheridan, took a tremendous tumble in the penalty area to give us a nerve-wracking climax to the end of the season. Under protest from the opposition, a penalty was duly awarded and, when we finally cleared the fans from the pitch, up stepped Neil Redfearn to take the most important kick of his career. It was the single best thing he has ever done on a footy pitch. He firmly planted the ball in the bottom right-hand of the net, and then there was another pitch invasion. I have the thing on video, and it is great to watch Paul Moulden wipe out a fan who ran into his celebration path. Then the news came in from Upton Park that the Hammers had been rolled over 2–0 and had started to celebrate because they thought that we had lost. The trophy was already down at their ground and had to be flown back up north for the following day's celebration. This time we had a meaningful open-top bus ride around Oldham, although I was asleep through most of it on account of a late evening and a lunchtime session on the Sunday prior to the excursion. To say that I was fried to the gills was an understatement – but why not? Most pro footballers go through their careers without winning a thing and I thought I was going to be one of them. It was, therefore, well worth celebrating. I could now wander the streets of my home town with my head held high. I was well aware of the next barrage of insults and knock-downs which I was about to face, though. This was launched at me from my detractors.

'Yeah, you've done well getting there in the last two seasons, but you won't survive in the big time.' They would say that it was okay playing these sides in the Cup competitions and turning them over at home, but it would be different in the League. 'And you won't have your plastic pitch to help you either.' This was true, as the authorities had ordered us to rip up our flexible friend, mainly because we were panning the sides of the establishment and the powers that be didn't like that. The pessimists only made me try harder and I was determined to succeed in the top division – on grass or plastic, it wouldn't matter to me. We had one issue to settle and that was a testimonial game for Roger Palmer, the Latics' all-time record goal scorer. Roger Palmer is worth some airspace. Quite simply he was a phenomenon, a total natural at what he did. His movement in the penalty area was perfect and the type of thing you try to coach all strikers to do. If you asked him to explain it, however, he would not be able to offer any insight into what he was doing. He could do it like a lion stalks its prey. It was impossible to wind him up because he just wouldn't respond. He was known as the 'Black Assassin', in that he often used to finish players off, and one of my most endearing memories of him was his collision with Neville Southall. The previous season's marathon Cup tie against Everton ended in typical Oldham controversy. The two incidents that I relate accurately sum up the Oldham character. The games against a belligerent Everton side, who were still under the impression that they were unstoppable, showed the true spirit in the Latics' side. We were never beaten and proved it time and again over the course of these games by coming back from the edge of defeat on several occasions. In the final game we had again gone a goal down, when suddenly inspiration occurred. An innocent-enough build-up created a one-on-one situation between 'mad Nev' and 'Oooh Roger Palmer' as he was known to the fans. The size and weight differences between these two were the equivalent of the mismatch of a lightweight against a heavyweight, or in this case rhino versus meerkat. The rhino charged out of his goal, only to be simultaneously confronted by the meerkat who, as we say in the trade, 'went through him' without flinching. Every time I see it I still can't get over the outcome, but the ball always ends in the net as the vet runs on to attend to the rhino. As a physio I can sympathise with the sponge man, as it is very difficult to treat wounded pride. This brought us back into the game, and it stumbled towards extra-time once again. There was more fortune as we were awarded a penalty at the end of the ground where the away fans congregate to sing their little hymns about player personalities. The spot-kick was to be taken by Ian Marshall, an ex-Evertonian and Britain's answer to Sir Les Patterson, and not a man to hide his feelings. The pent-up emotion of this Cup tie overflowed when he rammed the ball into the net, past a despairing Nev, and ran to greet his ex-fan club in the Rochdale Road end. Marshy sprinted up to the annoyed and depressed Scousers and then did something that would land him five weeks on the sidelines if he did it today. He performed a huge arcing run, giving animated two-fingered salutes to the gathering. You can imagine the reaction that this little gesture caused. That summed it up about us, though. Marshy and Roger showed the two sides to our spirit, bravery and fearlessness, with an underlying 'couldn't give a toss about what anyone thinks' attitude.

The game against Manchester City for Roger's testimonial was a fun affair played in good spirits, and we were still full of liquid spirit. Willie Donachie made us do an aerobic workout on the morning prior to the game and I'm sure I saw a champagne bubble emerge from Neil Adams's backside during one of the trickier movements. Before the game we had a team photo with the trophy, and myself and Marshy donned a pair of heavy metal rock star wigs. The thing was that in the printed picture, which was displayed in the *Oldham Evening Chronicle* the following day, you cannot tell that they are false hairdos, which tells you something about the state of our normal hair. We easily won the match, and Rodge pocketed a princely sum as the gate was over 15,000. The big question is – where is he now? No one seems to know. Even during his career, there was no knowledge of his general whereabouts. Willie picked up and dropped Roger off for a period of about 10 years but never knew where he lived, always just dropping him off at the end of some nameless street in Sale. The same went for picking him up. It was never outside his abode, but at the end of another road. That was the way at Oldham – on the way to an away game, usually down south, players were picked up en route at various convenient pick-up spots (convenient for both bus driver and player). Roger had several pick-up points and even at home I saw him just appear from behind a small terrace house opposite the ground. I imagined that he'd just slid down the drain pipe. So, where is the Rodge? Who knows? Wherever he is, he will remain forever one of Oldham's all-time heroes.

With the season finished and the mission accomplished I went for the usual summer break, which I again spent playing cricket. I also got married to Jean. We had bought a small terrace house in Skipton, which more or less needed completely gutting and starting from scratch. The project of marriage, doing up a dump and playing cricket kept me occupied during summer 1991, and before I knew it pre-season was around the corner. The wedding was a proper northern bash, from start to unconsciousness, and here are the key points. My wife, being a strict atheist, decided that we would tie the knot at Skipton registry office at 11am. This was horrific timing as the pubs don't open until that very hour, and there was no way I was going to go through the ordeal without a drop of Dutch courage inside me. Without it I would probably get cold feet and scratch the fixture at the last moment. Luckily, I knew the landlord of the Castle boozer, which was diagonally opposite the registry office at a distance of a good goal kick. When my best man, Melt, approached the landlord, Steve, he had no objection to opening up at 10am to let the festivities begin. Our dress code was 1920s and we descended en masse looking like the New York Mafia, to the surprise of many an early-morning shopper. At 10.55am Melt was standing as a lookout ready for the bride's arrival, whom we knew had a license to be late. 'No worries, she's bound to be late,' I mused, and we ordered our sixth pint. Suddenly it was red alert: the silly bugger had arrived two minutes ahead of schedule. I could only assume that the driver had dropped a clanger and mis-timed his approach. We had to down a full pint and leg it across to the point of no return. I'm usually fine in the 'downing' department, but on top of five recently swigged beers and the previous night's pay-load, a sudden sprint was not what the doctor ordered. Luckily, though, it was a false alarm: there must have been a wedding on at the parish church. There we were, then, some 20 minutes early – by 11 o'clock Jean hadn't even got her dress on. She's been like this ever since.

Following the ceremony we were driven 200 yards to the Black Horse for a champagne reception. This sounds lavish, but in truth I had saved up my Man of the Match awards (all two of them) over the last couple of years and then added to the collection with some top-quality fizzy wine. Family and close friends joined us to clear this drink for about an hour before two coaches arrived to take around a hundred guests up the Yorkshire Dales to the reception, held at the Fell Inn hotel at Burnsall. This place is elevated above the village, offering superb views across the valley or dale. Myself and my wife were driven there by our chauffeur for the day, Uncle Stewart, who was to come into his own later in the proceedings. Once the formalities of the photos and meal were over, everyone seemed to pick up the pace on the drinking front. By 6pm the scene reminded me more of an annual rugby club dinner than a wedding, and things were about to get worse.

We were all set to head back for Skipton when we realised that our driver, Uncle Stewart, who's like Bernard Manning only worse, wasn't capable of walking, never mind negotiating the windy Dales roads. We had to join the fray on the coaches, leaving the venue after four hours of drinking. Singing was soon cranked up to considerable decibels, and then the clothes-removal stage quickly followed. My wife's face told me all I needed know of what she thought of the proceedings, and I didn't dare allow my eyes come into contact with my mother's. We were on the second coach, which I thought was probably the most raucous of the two; however, I was wrong. The back window of the first coach was filled with arses, and not just male either. The choreographer of the art work in front was my best man, Melt, who has a particular talent in the field of performing arts. The afternoon had certainly degenerated, but now came the final act. Mel Rees, the cat-loving Welsh goalkeeper I mentioned in a previous chapter, took it upon himself to respond to the signal from the front vehicle. He had been born with the wedding tackle of a rogue elephant, and without so much of an 'excuse me Mrs…' he lowered his trousers and displayed his wares to the front coach and to everyone on ours. It wasn't just a discreet revealing, but a full tribal dance. Several aged relatives fainted, and I looked for that hole in the ground that's never there when you want it.

On arrival back in Skipton, the mob poured themselves into the local boozers. while the more respectable and aged guests retired to their hotels in a state of shock. It had been a long day, and it was a good job we had a couple of hours before the evening entertainment began. This interlude between reception and evening do may be regarded as half-time. At Mel's wedding the previous year in Cardiff, where I excelled myself by squirting a bloke's wig off with a soda syphon from the top of a balcony, Mel went out on the razzle during the interval with the lads, sending his wife back to the hotel on her own. It takes a certain amount of class to carry this off. In the evening we were joined by another 200 guests for a 1920s-style fancy dress at the Black Horse, which everyone entered into with tremendous gusto. There was a jazz band playing all the old hits and Melt had organised a cassette of all the best chart hits from our era, the late 1970s and early 80s. The Clifford Suite at the Black Horse was a veritable 'who's who' of football and a very enjoyable evening was had by all. It was mainly incident free, apart from Bouckley smashing a couple of optics behind the bar with a golf ball. His idea of fancy dress was to come as a 1920s golfer, complete with full equipment. At around 11pm, and no doubt heavily laced with sauce, he hit one of the balls with his mashie niblick. The missile went flying against the far wall, returning with a vengeance at a fairly rapid pace but at low altitude, and so it hit the carpet stay around the edge of the dance floor and looped up behind the bar into the optics. The bar staff were not too impressed with this trick. Still, a good day and night was had by all, and off I went with the wife, now to be known as the 'Dragon', to Sorrento, Italy, for the honeymoon. The only comment that I can make about this particular exercise was concerning the airport at Naples. The car park where we were picked up by the holiday company, which I found out was the only car park that they had, was so small that it rivalled Chesterfield Football Club for the world's smallest and most inadequate facility. It was ridiculously crammed, packed with cars and buses and irritable people shouting, gesticulating and sounding their horns.

Pre-season loomed and I decided to return to my roots to get fit before I arrived back at the club. As the management had said, if we went back fit we would be able to spend more time on the training field and less time yomping on Saddleworth Moor. This stretched the truth somewhat. As I mentioned, I was desperate to do well to shove the criticism up my detractors' backsides, so fitness was a priority. I did some fell-running up Embsay Crag, which is a very gruelling way of getting fit, but extremely effective. Afterwards you'd walk like John Wayne for a few days, but it enabled me to get through the bleep test on the first day easily enough. A bleep test is a speed-endurance exercise, which strictly speaking should not be done in the first week of pre-season training and is not much more than a measure of one's ability to run 20 metres and get a good turn in against a progressively increasing metronome. For those of you who are not familiar with this kind of torture, about 10 of you participate, running alongside each other and dropping out when they fail to keep up with speed. At the beginning it is very slow and you can reach the 20 metre point and turn well before the beep, so timing is the key. Each time it goes up a gear, a voice tells you the next level has been reached and everyone has to speed up to keep time. An acceptable level is level 12, but that is not really adequate and it should be more like 15. Occasionally you would see someone's breakfast in spectacular fashion, but it didn't really bother me. Stuff like this, constant stopping and starting, was tailor-made for my position on the field. Lightweight players fared far better than tall and heavy lads, and as I got older the test became harder. There were other exercises more suited to players like me then, such as the standing long jump or the sit and reach hamstring stretch. Thankfully it was what you did on the pitch that counted with Joe, in the early days at least. Pre-season was very exacting at Oldham, and it was important that you did well so as to make the pre-season tour to Scandinavia or some such place. When you're a pro you are on show all the time, not just during a game, and I have been dropped for a game on the basis of how I appeared during the week, or at least that's what they said to me anyway. Thus, Willie Donachie did everything he could to test the lads and ensure that those who survived were very fit. An early-morning swim at eight o'clock was followed by running on the moors at 9.30am, or some speed endurance in a north Manchester park, or the bleep test in the gym. In the afternoon we'd return to the ground for some football work, which is not easy when your legs are like jelly. I began to get a bit paranoid about my weight as they used to weigh us most mornings before we exercised, so I used to get up for a 40-minute run at 5am and put a bin bag next to my skin to help me sweat so I would be lighter at the weigh-in. A quick shower, back to bed for another hour, then up again and off to training at seven in the morning. It sounds torturous but there are very good reasons for this madness and for the obsessive concern about weight. An early-morning start meant an early night and no pub, so that the fitness would build instead of being ruined by alcohol. The excessive, Spartan-like regime also ensured that we players were too knackered to contemplate anything other than sleep of an evening, and it worked. The weight issue is more technical, although I'm not sure how many coaches are fully aware of its implications. There is a physiological measurement called the Max V02, which is greatly affected by a person's body fat value almost to the point of being directly proportional. It is the amount of oxygen the body can consume in litres per minute per kilogram. In the sports world the largest figures are found among cross-country skiers, followed by marathon runners and tri-athletes. Soccer players have to have good values, with rugby less so, although that is changing. Lower figures are found with cricketers and golfers. Darts and snooker require you to be barely alive in order to play the games, and in the early televised days of these events, when the likes of Alex Higgins and Bill Werbeniuk were the stars, one would have found negative figures with most of the competitors due to the amount of fags and booze they consumed.

Fitness being addressed, off we went in July 1991 to Sweden. I had always dreamt of going on a pre-season tour to somewhere like this ever since I got into the pro game. Previously, pre-season had consisted of visiting exotic places such as

Seaton Carew and Peterlee, and those two never-to-be-forgotten tours of the south-west with Watford, but now, finally, I was seeing something of the world, courtesy of my profession. I quickly worked out why Scandinavia is a popular place for football clubs in July. It's an ideal place to play friendlies because it has plenty of highly fit semi-professional teams that you can hammer out of sight but who keep going until the end (and it's jam-packed with gorgeous women). The Swedes and Norwegians can certainly organise things when it comes to sport and no expense seemed to be spared. On one visit we were heading up a mountain range on the way to our training camp, and I can distinctly remember commenting that there couldn't possibly be a pitch in this region as it was practically sheer. Then, out of the blue, we turned the corner and there was the pitch, literally carved sideways out of the mountain. They had blasted the pitch out of the rock face, and what a superb set-up it was. I made enquiries as to what the deal was, as inside there was a full fitness centre and gymnasium. I thought it must have belonged to some big set-up or team, but no, it was just a facility for the local village of about 3,000 people. It made our stuff back home in Oldham look sick. That is the way in those countries – you pay through the nose for everything and are heavily taxed, but you certainly get it back in the investments the local and central government make. People accept this and alter their lifestyles in order to counteract this high standard of living. It's not all good news, however, and there is a price to pay for this. They have a very high suicide rate in Scandinavia, and when I'd ordered a round of drinks after a game I felt like hanging myself. The price of drinks is scandalous and it makes our breweries in Britain look like they're giving it away. It got so ridiculous that we had to start paying by credit card, and to combat the problem of having to take out a mortgage to pay for your ale, the Swedes stay in getting pissed on cheap plonk until 11pm and then descend upon the streets to pick up whatever specimen takes their fancy. They even go across to Denmark on the ferry to alleviate the expenses. If it works out cheaper to get wazzed on a boat and spend a few hours in a foreign country than to stroll down to the local to down a couple of pints, then you've got serious problems. After a good pre-season in Sweden, in which we played and won six games, scoring 31 goals, we returned ready for the top flight.

Although pro footballers work very hard, they do undoubtedly have a lot of time on their hands. Traditionally this was spent in the bookies, at the racecourse and down the pub, but it also leaves plenty of time for practical jokes and the correction of such incidents: revenge. During pre-season the previous summer I had the misfortune to nod off during a drinking debacle over the border in Ripponden, Mexico. We called it Mexico because of its sanctuary from the all-seeing eyes of the gaffer. Joe Royle had his network of spies and informers around Oldham and north Manchester, but the radar ran out once we crossed the border into Yorkshire. We could get away with far more over there, such as going out for a quiet pint and not seeing it reported in the papers the next day, and it was a positive disaster to go out in Oldham. One evening I had fallen asleep while under the influence of the nectar in the Fleece and awoke to find that half my hair was hacked off. As I had particularly long locks at the time it did look ridiculous. The thing was that we were due in training that very morning and I couldn't do much about it. I turned out looking like Jim off *Taxi* on one profile and Lemmy out of Motorhead on the other. I could see it perturbed the manager a great deal, but he didn't say anything. There was only one thing for it, so after I had had the piss ripped from my soul I disappeared to a local barber in Springhead to have the damage shorn down to the wood. I then looked like an internee of Alcatraz for the start of the season. I couldn't resist the opportunity to make immediate use of this new look to pull a pre-season spoof with the new hairdo.

We had signed a new 'keeper, John Keeley, and I twigged that none of the fans would have yet seen him, so I donned his goalie shirt and ran out for a warm-up before the game against Bradford City. Of course, nobody recognised my new look and I received a small ovation from the fans, which is the universal welcome to any new player. It took them a good while to twig that it was me in the nets.

You'd have thought that anyone with any sense would use their time to great effect, such as going to university in the afternoon, or taking up a night class and studying Spanish, or anything, but not our lot. The nearest pub or snooker hall was the first port of call. Then, under the influence, the practical jokes would be conceived. I am sure that this is where the plan to cut my hair was born, and they just waited for the right moment. So now, with too much time on my hands – I had already done the university bit twice – I set about my revenge. I had narrowed the culprits down to Melt, Phil Brown, Nick Henry and Mike Milligan and set about plotting my plan of attack. I decided to pick them off one by one – maybe I'd seen too many spaghetti westerns – in order to complete the task thoroughly. The first was Phil, whom I had arranged to meet after our first game of the season away to Wolverhampton Wanderers. We met in Halifax at 8pm and my task was straightforward enough as I knew his mind very well. He is an amateur psychologist and one of the best at playing mind games that I have come across. Because of this, he is highly suspicious of anything out of the ordinary and is constantly on his guard. I had to get enough alcohol down him that he lost his concentration, but not so much that I lost him. Phil had the habit of doing a Captain Oates when full, and he would announce that he was going to the toilet or just for a burger or some other such excuse and that would be the last that you would see of him. It was a balmy summer's evening and we were standing outside in Halifax town centre watching all the people go by. After our fourth pint I declared that I was hungry, and this seemed to strike a chord with Phil.

'I fancy a "Spud-u-like" what d'you reckon?'

'Yeah, good idea. I'll go get them,' said Phil.

'No, I'll get them, you get the beers in,' I said. 'What do you want on yours?' He opted for garlic chicken topping, and I decided on the same so as to add some stability to his mind. If I'd have gone for something completely different he would have checked his food meticulously as it would have been easy to doctor it. I arrived with the sustenance and handed the grub to him. Now his mind was in overdrive and I could see the beads of sweat on his brow. He finally made a decision and reached out past the one on offer and took mine. This was a stroke of luck as I had planned on this eventuality. Seconds later he was plowing into his grub like he hadn't been fed for a week. Suddenly, he went white and twitched. 'WHAT the...Oh God...You...Bastard man...' He staggered and dropped his food. Then he started coughing like he was going to be sick. He gagged and spat out onto his hand and there it was, the culprit – my big toenail. One of the by-products of soccer is a copious supply of sloughed-off dry skin and blackened toenails from the relentless hammering they take from July to May. I had a classic blackened nail, complete with yellow slime and green fungus, and it stunk like nothing on earth. Brown ran off in the direction of the big white telephone, making the mistake of leaving the offending article on the pavement. Without a second thought, I retrieved the nail and popped into his pint and it conveniently sank. Brown returned saying things like 'very good' and 'very funny', and generally it was smiles all round until he finished his pint and choked the thing back into his gob. The reaction was less dramatic but nonetheless pleasing to me. Although I didn't think this to be severe enough punishment for cutting a man's hair, it would have to do for now.

Next in line was Melt. Being a teacher he would be out in mid-afternoon and this left a perfect window of opportunity in which to visit his house and sabotage something. He had been constructing a patio, which was to become an obsession and his pride and joy. Thing was, it was pink and yellow squares, a most revolting mixture. At the time I was living in that small Civil War cottage, and the heating was generated by a wood-burning stove connected to the central heating. When I'd finally cranked the stove up to its full output potential, you didn't need the central heating. The heat output alone would be enough to singe your eyebrows at 10 feet. The trouble was that it created bin bag after bin bag of ash, and this had to be removed as typically the bin men wouldn't do it. Mainly I used to take it with me to Oldham and drop it in one of the skips around the back of the club. Then I had a brainwave – why not drop it off at Melt's on the way home? Well, it's not strictly on the way home, but going to Skipton via Bradford from Oldham is not too inconvenient. And what better place than on his patio? I delivered the first batch of soot to Melt's pride and joy and continued for the rest of the week. I knew that he would not see it until the weekend because he went to work in the dark and came back in the dark, but when he did see it – what a reaction! Not from him so much, but from his wife, Alison. It completely threw him and he couldn't work out who had done it. He started accusing his neighbours and a few of his local soccer team, but never put the equation together implicating me. The most amusing thing to me was that after an hour's scrubbing with Vim and hot water, the stain was still present in a huge circle and is to this day as a bit of a reminder.

Milligan and Henry were easier to deal with and required far less involved plans. I preyed on their most potent phobia and for many pro footballers it is the same. This is their totally irrational fear of shit. In fact, pro footballers have a fear of anything studenty. I first noticed this problem at Halifax when I released a chocolate submarine from the depths during a post-training relaxation session in the communal bath. You should have seen the lads move. They did a brilliant Harrier Jump Jet impersonation as they collectively levitated themselves vertically out of the water in horror. The submarine and I had a good old relax together for a while afterwards.

I chose Sweden as the ideal place to exact my revenge on the lads as this was the ideal time to surprise them because their guard was down. When on international trips, especially in places like Sweden, with the foreign air and romantic spirit, the lads often become complacent and vulnerable. Our toilet was blocked and I decided to use a bucket in the corner of the room and used water to damp down the smell. The 'Captain' wasn't too impressed and was clucking his disapproval around the hotel room like Foghorn Leghorn, but he couldn't do anything about it because he couldn't stand the smell. I left the cocktail to ferment and went out on the razzle following a game. As the night drew to a close I sneaked off early and took up my vantage position on the third-floor balcony of the hotel. The night club that the victims were to emerge from was next door and so the location couldn't have been better. There I was, like a modern-day Quasimodo, ready to pour boiling oil on his enemies below, only in this case it was liquid shit. Just as I was about to eject the contents on my victims below, I was spotted by Mike Milligan, who is always on the lookout for trouble. I missed my opportunity, and the lads ran into the sanctuary of the hotel. Now it was a guessing game – which floor would they ascend to, their own or one above or below and then use the steps? I figured that either way they would have to pass the lift door on their own floor so that is where I waited. Unbelievably they emerged at their own level, and as the doors slid apart they were at my mercy, all three of them. Mike Milligan, Neil Adams and Graeme Sharpe looked in horror as I drew back the bucket and launched the contents into the lift. They attempted to duck and then fled like the wind. Then the full horror of the event struck me with the mess that I had created inside the lift. I had better clean it, I thought, or I would get deported. I started a cleanathon which was to take me two hours, and what made it worse was that I couldn't get the lift to stay put. I ended up travelling up and down in the lift, cleaning it from 2am until 4am, which is not the easiest thing to do when you've had a few. Unfortunately, as no doubt you've noticed, a couple of innocents got dragged into the fray in Adams and Sharpe, and Henry seems to have escaped. Henry did get it in the end, but the tale is not printable.

After the antics of the pre-season, there we were in the old First Division and we were ready to rumble with the best. We had signed Sharpe from Everton to bolster the attack and Brian Kilkline from Coventry to head the ball out of the stadium. Brian, or 'Bwian' as he was to become known (instantly recognisable to all Monty Python fans), provided us all with a comic moment by becoming the only player in history to go down with cramp inside the first 10 minutes of a pre-season friendly in Sweden. What had he been doing?

We shocked Liverpool by taking the lead at Anfield on the opening day of the season but then blew several chances and lost 2–1. We only had a couple of days to wait until our first points of the season, though, when we hammered Chelsea 3–0 at home. It was made more pleasurable because Dennis Wise was playing. I thundered in a half-volley which Dave 'Lurch' Beasant never saw, and we were liberated. The season was a great learning experience for us and for me in particular in that I had to get used to being dropped occasionally, sometimes deserved, sometimes not. I learned that I could terrorise the First Division defences, and despite being dropped I easily achieved top assists man in all League football for season 1991–92. In other words more goals were created by me than any other player that year. Did it get me any recognition apart from the info appearing in *Match Magazine* and *Shoot*? Did it buggery! My name had been bandied about for England, and appearing for England B was a distinct possibility, but I was completely overlooked by the establishment, and when Chris Waddle and John Barnes got injured and couldn't go to Sweden for the Euro '92 Championships, who did they select? Andy Sinton. A right-sided player brought in to supply crosses from the left wing. I've nothing against Andy, but he's never been to the by-line and pulled a cross back for the centre-forward in his life. He always cut in-field and played to feet. Consequently, he never got a cross in during the tournament, in which England were sent packing very early on. The whole tour had been a debacle from start to finish.

That is my one regret in life – that I never got chance to play for England. When I look at some of the players who have I could cry. I did not have great pace – neither did Beckham – but I could do my job, and some of the players I see now make me despair. When I see some of the players appearing for the other Home Nations because their grandfather was born there, that makes me sick as well. I could trace back my Irish ancestry but couldn't be arsed, because if I could not play for England then tough. I didn't want to play for anyone else. Some of my colleagues went on to win lots of caps for their countries, and good luck to them, but how many could call themselves international class? It's also a shame for the really good lads for countries like Wales and Northern Ireland as they are marooned in qualifiers and friendlies and never get the opportunity to ply their stuff on the world stage.

That first season in the top flight had been good for Oldham and, although we finished 17th in the League, we were comfortable and had played well. What's more, with my top assists man accolade, I could stick two fingers up at everyone.

By now I was studying physiotherapy at Salford University and spent my summer in a hospital on placement while my teammates were in Florida. The season had been fairly incident-free, but one game did take the biscuit and caused me to question my future at the club. We were playing that great under-achiever from north London, Spurs, at home, and though we were dominating the game, it was goalless as the half-time whistle blew. We were then subjected to boos and whistles of derision from our own fans. I couldn't believe it. Here we were playing top-grade football in the town for the first time in 67 years and entertaining supposed household names, and we got booed off for drawing 0–0 at half time. We subsequently won 1–0, but it didn't stop me from lambasting the fans to a reporter. I said that the fans were morons and didn't deserve top-flight football in the town. The following morning I was rudely awoken from my slumber by Joe, who was to the point, as usual. 'Morning, Wur, have you seen the papers? Go out and get one and ring me in 10 minutes.'

I ambled down to the paper shop and purchased a good old selection of that highbrow Sunday morning literature that we English are so keen on. When I turned the *Sunday People* over I could have died. There, in the largest type available to the publisher, was the word 'MORONS' spread all the way across the back page. Underneath was a picture of yours truly in Oldham battle regalia alongside a write-up of my comments and a small report on the game. I rang back and said words to the effect of, 'What's wrong with that?' This brought a stifled laugh from the big man, and he calmly advised me to be careful who I talked to after the matches. It was no secret that Joe Royle did not see eye-to-eye with several of the academics in popular journalism (and still doesn't), in particular the southern ones. He reckoned that they did not give a true representation of Oldham Athletic and portrayed us as only being where we were due to the plastic pitch, believing that we would soon be heading back to the depths of Division Two without our flexible friend.

I had decided enough was enough and had begun to think of moving on. I knew interest was keen and so I waited patiently to the end of the season, which was to be the last-ever in the old structure of the Football League. Gone forever was the First Division as we knew it, to be replaced by the Premier League, which was effectively the same League, only with more money and a different name. Interestingly enough, I've never met a pro footballer who thought it was a good idea, and I still have my doubts as to whether it will end in tears or not. No doubt some of the lads who earn in excess of £90,000 a week quite like it, though it has probably got worse for the lads who play for the smaller clubs, and that needs to be considered.

Summer 1992 was spent in Otley and Airedale General hospitals on placement for my physiotherapy course, practising all the various treatments of all the conditions I'd learned about during my first year. The curious thing I found was that when I learnt about a new condition, I'd suffer the symptoms myself for about a week. Every night-sweat and pimple was attributed to the latest disease on the scene. At the end of the summer Jean and I went off to San Francisco for a fortnight to see my cousin, and I took the opportunity to do some running in the heat on the slopes of a distinctly suspicious looking mountain called Mount Diabolo, which got me as fit as I had been at the end of the season. It was an eye-opening experience living in San Fran. It's a totally different way of life to the one I had been used to. It's an ideal place to get fit, as they don't have a local that you can just wander down to in an evening for a few pints; most restaurants and bars need driving to. When I returned, there was still no real news of a move and so I geared myself for another season with Oldham which, to be honest, I was quite looking forward to. The pre-season training went well. I was fit enough and things were good on the playing side until we met Barnsley in a pre-season game at Oakwell. We were comprehensively stuffed 3–1, and not surprisingly Joe saw red. His anger was quite exacting and I decided to respond, causing him to question why I suddenly had a lot to say. I retorted with the fact that I hadn't said much because I hadn't needed to say much in the last three years. I could see his point at being angry with me because I warmed up with a flat cap on, which was hardly the height of professionalism; however, it was merely my way of getting at the Barnsley fans with a touch of humour, or so I thought, and I wanted to get back at them for the last few visits. Perhaps I was wrong to have a go, as Joe did seem somewhat over-stimulated. I was more angry with the way we were going as a team and as a club than anything else. Looking back now, I realise that this should have been of little concern to me, but as I had put my heart and soul into the club, I felt I was more a part of it than merely an employee or asset. We were a shadow of ourselves from two years before, when we were feared by all the big clubs in the land. Why were we selling all our best players, especially with all the money we had made in the last few seasons? Dennis Irwin, Mike Milligan, Earl Barrett, Paul Warhurst and Neil Redfearn were all sold for good money, but I felt sure we would have been better off upgrading their contracts and not wasting the money on more expensive and yet inferior subjects. What was in 1990–91 a very solvent club with a great future was on the verge of bankruptcy by 1999 and on the football slag heap. I could see it coming, and when myself and Ian Marshall were sold a few days after the Barnsley friendly, this was more evidence of the direction we were going in. It is no surprise, though, when you examine the types of brains of most football directors and chairmen. Shackleton, the ex-Sunderland player, got it right when in his book he had a chapter on the knowledge of football directors and left a single blank page.

I sloped off home from this Barnsley game, almost two years after Longy's fateful day when I was last at Barnsley, and decided that it was not a good idea to ever sign for them. I'd had enough shit there just on visits, and the prospect of going there every day was not one I relished. Several days later I left Oldham, but not to join Barnsley.

# five

# In the Lebanon

One morning in late July 1992 I was sitting in my bar having a cup of coffee ready to go to training when the phone rang. It was Joe, who told me to stay close to the blower as Peter Reid was about to call me from Italy. Sure enough, he did and by tea time, after having passed through my medical, I was a Manchester City player in a collective £1.2 million deal involving two players, Neil Pointon and Steve Redmond, going in the opposite direction. Apparently I was worth £900,000 plus two players, which came to the £1.2 million package. Well what do you know? From Burnley reject to this was quite a story. I was told to get my stuff, including my passport, and get to Manchester. I went into Maine Road to train on my own and then to catch a plane to Milan in order to meet up with the team, who were on a pre-season tour. I did some speed work with Terry Darracott, City's equivalent of Tom Whalley in that he had an outrageous limp, and then rushed off to Ringway. This was the life – jet-setting across Europe to meet the team on tour, having signed a nice four-year contract. What glamour, what class, what a flaming drag. The flight, in bog-standard punter-class seats, was okay, about two and a half hours, and gave me chance to reflect on this very theme. I was informed that there would be someone at the airport to meet me when I arrived. I imagined a posh car and a chauffeur, maybe even a limo, to take me the small distance to the hotel.

When I emerged through customs, I searched the panorama for an important-looking bloke to take me forward. All I could find was a small blond-haired chap in denims, smoking a fag and holding up a piece of cardboard saying 'Holden'. This had to be a piss-take, but what choice did I have? We shook hands and I followed him out to the car park, which at Milan is slightly larger than Naples, and again I made the mistake of thinking way above my station. No limo, no large saloon car, not even a good-looking vehicle. He walked up to the worst piece of junk in sight and I looked around for Jeremy Beadle. It was a battered old light blue three-door Fiat 127 the size of a baked bean tin. The inside was covered in a litter of old newspapers and cigarette packets, and Ronnie Corbett would have been squashed up in terms of leg room. Off we went and we got chatting away about this and that, and it turned out that this bloke was just a fan who had said to Peter Reid that he would be in Milan at the time of my arrival and would therefore pick me up. He could have been anybody, he could have kidnapped me and I could have spent the next 15 months tied to a radiator in the Middle East. And boy, was it hot. It felt like the Arabian peninsula and there wasn't a chance that this contraption had air conditioning. My only forms of cooling were to wind the window down, but that only let in hot air, and to drink half a bottle of warm water, which at least replaced the fluid I was losing at an alarming rate. The mad fan, called Chris I think, then said the journey would take another two and a half hours, at which point I suddenly felt hungry, tired, too hot and really pissed off. We were heading for the blasted Dolomites, a fact given away by the steady incline and dangerous, winding roads. On and on we went, climbing higher and higher, getting hotter and hotter. After an age we arrived high in the stratosphere at a cute Italian village surrounded by mountains. It was the Italian equivalent of Machu Picchu. I de-cramped myself from the tin can and, for what reason I'll never know, thanked the driver, who had also done his level best to bore me shitless about Italy and Manchester City, and then approached the hotel. Suspiciously, to one side there was a team coach fully laden with lads looking like footy players on the way to a game. I thought that it couldn't possibly involve me, or that maybe they had just got back from somewhere. Then, as if ejected by some clever mechanism, Peter Reid flew out from the side of the bus with an outstretched hand. 'All right der lad, put yer stuff in the foyer, get yer boots and come and join us,' he said, as if trying to impersonate one of the Beatles.

Bloody hell, I thought, what's happening? I enquired and found out that we were due to play Verona that very evening in a friendly, and that the ground was two and a half hours down the road. I couldn't believe this, we were retracing the hell I had just endured, only this time I was with a bunch of strangers instead of one tedious bloke. To make it worse, we were going downhill now. One false move by the driver and we'd be history on the side of an Italian mountain. To get to Verona from where we were, you go to Milan and turn left, which we did and arrived the customary hour before kick-off. Thankfully I was on the bench and didn't feel too bad after the warm-up by Sam Ellis, the assistant manager. It mirrored the warm-up style at Watford, which was not surprising as Sam was at Watford with Taylor for a few years. I began to get the impression of the club and the characters involved in it and immediately hit it off with Steve McMahon, Niall Quinn and Tony Coton, whom I knew from Watford. There were a couple that I was instantly suspicious of in Keith Curle and Fitzroy Simpson, but the rest seemed okay. The only other staff were the physio, Eammon Salmon, and the old wily fox, Tony Book, who were both fairly genial.

Midway through the first half, Paul Lake, who was trying to recover from an anterior cruciate ligament injury, got hurt and I was asked to warm up. Very soon I was thrown on and received a nice reception from the travelling City faithful among whom, no doubt, was my driver. The first pass to me was from full-back Ian Brightwell, whose parents were both international runners, and he must have thought that I was some sort of wonder athlete too. The ball was behind me and at pace, causing me to check my stride and try to hook my foot around it to keep it in play. Unfortunately the pill got stuck under my ankle and down I went, taking the ball with me into touch. What a start: £1.2 million for that! The game drifted on and petered out into a 0–0 draw. The only other thing I can remember about it was big Quinny complaining that I was crossing the ball before he got into the box. The facilities were good at the ground and put a lot of English clubs to shame at the time. For instance, they had an outdoor 400m running track and an underground indoor 400m track for training, for when it was too hot, I supposed. The atmosphere inside the stadium was electric and reminded me of a scaled-down version of Wembley. Following the game we went back up into the Alps and finally, after some appetising Italian cuisine consisting of thin slices of ham and cheese with holes in and some featureless pasta, I managed to get my head down and get some rest. What a day, but what would tomorrow bring?

I needn't have worried about it being quiet and incident-free. We had more boring continental food for breakfast – I was sick of it after one day – and then training was on the front lawn of the hotel at 10.30am. This was fine and nothing that I hadn't seen before at Oldham or Watford. In the afternoon the lads just milled about, some sunbathing, others playing pitch and putt on the small course that they had at this beautiful mountain resort. In the evening we headed up the mountain to entertain a small village team who, like the Swedes, had chiselled the pitch from out of the rock face. It was one of those one-way-traffic games where you lost count of how many goals you'd scored before half-time. Italian amateurs are as bad as any other country and have ridiculous kits like their English counterparts. Following the game we were treated like royalty and the gaffer declared that we would all go out for a meal and then have a drink. A respectable restaurant was found in the small town and we sat down to more pasta, only this time with venison and some tomato. Soon after the lads broke out into song, led by David White, the very speedy winger. They were taking it in turn to sing these songs, which were mainly classics from the 1950s and 1960s, such as *American Pie*, and then all the chaps would join in with the popular chorus. Well this was strange and definitely a new one on me in the footy world. The only experience I'd previously had of this, apart from at cub scouts, was at my old 'trousers down' rugby union club, Wharfedale. It soon got around to my turn, as I knew it would, and I had been searching the old memory for a song that might fit in. I could not think of anything appropriate, mainly because I didn't know any of those types of songs. I told the lads that I was at a loss, but Sam replied, 'Come on, you have to sing one song. It's compulsory as a new member of the squad to sing us a song.' Again, I tried to protest my ignorance and began to wonder what I'd been doing all my life if I couldn't think of at least one mundane popular song. Then it came to me:

Oh the seagulls they fly high in Mobile,

Oh the seagulls they fly high in Mobile,

Oh the seagulls they fly high,

And they shite right in your eye,

It's a good job pigs can't fly in Mobile!

In Mobile in Mobile in Mo in Mo in Mo in Mobile

Oh the seagulls they fly high and they shite right in your eye

It's a good job pigs can't fly in Mobile!


Well I knew that would soften them. Stunned silence greeted the end of the rendition and looks of incredulity all around. Peter Reid fell about laughing, while the serious singers like Dave White and Big Sam still looked as if they'd been told that their wives had just run off with Peter Beardsley and Iain Dowie. The chorus was easy enough, so I couldn't understand why they didn't join in. Still, it did the trick – I was never asked to sing again. The evening wore on as we moved from bar to bar in small groups. I had found myself in a nice school of quaffers in Quinny, TC (Tony Coton), Macca and Big Sam. We had a jolly old evening, which was only marred by another classic from yours truly. In an attempt to break up a misunderstanding between Quinny and Macca, I was knocked off-balance in a shopping mall. I came to an abrupt stop against a huge shopfront window and bounced off. The thing made a huge 'boww' sound as it flung me clear. Then…SMASH. Down it went into a million pieces. What a noise. You've never heard anything like it. The arcade acoustics amplified it by a dozen times and it must have been audible all around the Dolomites, possibly causing the odd avalanche. The two protagonists fled in opposite directions like a couple of naughty schoolboys while Big Sam grabbed me and rushed me back inside into the bar. During the episode I had been carrying my huge stein with me, which contained two litres of Eurofizz lager, and I was proud to say that I didn't spill a drop. Then, like sharks around a carcass, the cops arrived dressed for war with their batons and guns. It's a good job that I was back inside the bar or I would have been dragged off into the night for an evening inside. We made our way quietly back to the hotel and sneaked off to bed. At eight the following morning Sam poked his head around the door and informed me that the gaffer wanted to interview me. Steve McMahon was my roomy, and he just let out a quiet chuckle. I got dressed and made my way around to the boss's room. I knocked and entered the room, which must have been the largest in the hotel. Reidy was sitting behind a desk with his back to the early morning sunshine. I couldn't see his face. He must have watched lots of Westerns to know this tactic.

'Yous only been 'ere five minutes and you've fallen through a window, had the local cops wanting to press charges for wrecking their town, and yous caused two grand's worth of damage.' I knew that it was pointless trying to make excuses because footballers don't deal in excuses for things like this. I simply said that I was sorry and asked what I could do to help. 'Go and see all the lads and get £50 off each of them to pay for the damage.'

You can picture the scene. There I was, still considerably goose-eyed, minging to be precise, faced with the task of rounding up two grand's worth of Italian lira at 8am. Easy that. Just knock on a hotel bedroom door and ask the chap whom you only met in the last 24 hours for £50 because you were stupid enough to fall through a window in town. Fortunately, the football fraternity is genuinely noble at these coughing-up gestures, as it's better to give the money to hush up an incident than to pursue the angles of blame only to see more shit build up around your ears. Nothing more was said of the incident and thankfully it escaped the back pages of the press. The rest of the tour passed quietly, the only other talking point being a game against another Italian village team in which David White managed to miss an open goal and in the process hit both posts and the crossbar in one shot.

Back in Blighty we prepared to enter the brand new Premier League with all its hype and glamour. We were the first-ever Sky *Monday Night Football* hosts as we entertained QPR at Maine Road. It was soccer, American style, I thought, as there were pompom girls flashing their behinds at the crowd during the warm-up, cameras everywhere to capture every possible angle, and even fireworks at the end of the game. It was the beginning of the all-intrusive eye, allowing us to see what the goal would have looked like from where Fred Bloggs would have been standing.

STONEFIELD ST. SURGERY
STONEFIELD STREET
MILNROW, ROCHDALE.
LANCS. OL16 4JQ

Dr. STEPHEN P. ROTHERY
Dr. ANDREW J. PENROSE
Dr. JENNIFER A. GOLLAND
Dr. MARGARET H. OGDEN

Telephone:
*Appointments:* (0706) 46234
*Gen. Enquiries:* (0706) 50355
Fax: (0706) 527946

Mr. J. Royle,
Oldham Athletic Football Club,
Sheepfoot Lane,
Oldham.

20th April, 1994.

Dear Joe,

Following my recent communication, I believe Rick tried to contact me here at the surgery and I was unavailable. This is a pity as I feel I owe an explanation.

Some weeks ago I received some information (from a generally reliable source) and have since been in a quandary as what to do next. Please try to put yourself in my situation. Was I to keep silent upon an issue which might have a considerable impact on the team or was an annonymous letter in order? I felt the latter a cowardly way and so thought a direct approach to you to be most appropriate. My thoughts were for the club and not in any way meant as a malicious attack. If my source was mistaken in identifying Rick for a similarly appearing person then I own my heartfelt apologies to both of you. As, I hope, an honourable person, I am only too happy to accept this explanation of events.

You must appreciate that a senseless escalation of this issue can only be damaging to all parties concerned - excepting the legal people. As a long standing fan who worships the ground Rick and the lads stand on I appeal to your renowned good sense and nature to rapidly resolve this issue.

Please feel free to contact me at my surgery. Best wishes to the lads for tonight.

Yours sincerely,

Stephen P. Rothery.

**Having a good run.**                    **A long-haired 1970s-style picture.**

**My return to Oldham from Manchester City. Why did they make us do this?**

A fresh-faced pre-season photograph at Oldham. Was I starting to conform?

The celebration of my mazy solo goal against Leeds United in the Littlewoods League Cup game of 1989.

A sprint with Andy looking on. Check out Sheffield United's minging kit.

**I'm off on one. Nick Henry looks on, concerned.**

**Action from our first season back in the top flight in 1991.**

**It looks like I'm elbowing Paul Stewart in the face. Gary Mabbutt looks nonplussed.**

Christ only knows what I'm doing. Mick Milligan wonders, too, and Gary Mabbut looks surprised.

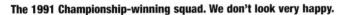

The 1991 Championship-winning squad. We don't look very happy.

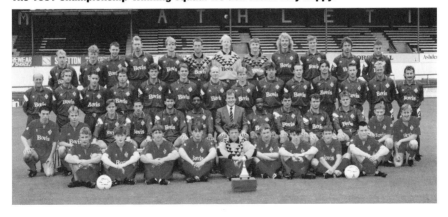

A long-range effort against Tranmere. Look at the technique – 'head down, son'.

Andy Ritchie gets a bear hug – he must have scored again.

A tussle with Portsmouth in 1994. I scored two penalties in the same place, a double bluff, and we won. Joe Royle left and I hardly ever started a game again after this.

Scoring a perfectly good, but
ruled out, header on my Oldham
home debut against Watford. I had
scored earlier. The referee took a
thorough look at me.

Sprinting against Stoke.

Graeme Sharp and I in our first
season back in the top flight.

Open top bus ride through Oldham after losing the 1990 League Cup Final. I couldn't see the point in this and hated every minute. It inspired me to win the League and promotion the following season, though.

Beating Manchester City for Oldham in 1994 and receiving the Okell's Brewery Trophy with Nick Henry.

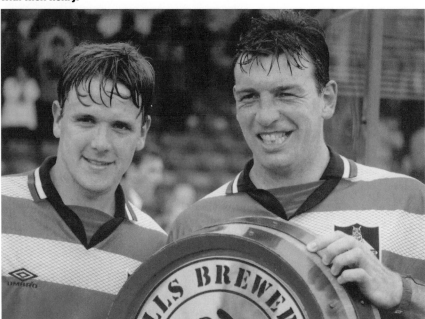

A northern training ground scene. Left to right: Joe, Darren Beckford, myself, Andy Barlow and Mark Brennan.

About to deliver at Maine Road.

Breathing out of my arse at Manchester City.

A pat from young Garry Flitcroft.

At City balancing a tarantula on my head.

**More old blokes' footy for Sky to make money off.**

**John Aldridge tries to score but we have him.**

**Winning the British Masters Football in 2003, the first major trophy for Manchester City since 1976. We had to prove that we could still do it.**

**Success at Peel winning the Manx FA Cup in 2007.**

Waving goodbye at Oldham in 1995, a great journey coming to an end.

Steve McMahon and I in Japan with Manchester City in 1993.

A golf day at Skipton Golf Club, Embsay. The crag is in background.

Myself and Andy Ritchie share the Man of the Match award for the first leg of the League Cup semi-final at home to West Ham. We won 6–0 and it became known as the St Valentine's Day Massacre.

At the family home at Peel in the Isle of Man. William is off on a sprint, Alex is in the pram, Jean is on the left, my sister Jen is in the middle and her husband Steve is sitting.

Three generations – Grandpa George (Wurpa), my dad, Rodge, and me, in Embsay.

Alex getting to grips with a ball at my Aunty Irene's house in Colne. His second cousin, Daniel, looks on, mistakenly wearing a Manchester United shirt.

**Myself and Maurice Powell on top of my iconic Silver Mountain in Embsay. This was the start of my hat-wearing days...**

Peel City, the best place on the Isle of Man.

The new concept of Premier League and Monday night football basically meant that there would be more football, which would be a little more jazzed up in its presentation, and the television people would plough lots more cash into the top-flight game. The clubs were bound to go for it. There is no evidence that the product is any better than it was 30 years ago, however, because the national side is still second rate and the domestic game is still producing the same winners. There is no change in the hierarchy of English football. The top sides 30 years ago are still at the top of the tree, give or take the odd sleeping giant, and the bottom sides are still bottom.

It was enjoyable to play in the all-new Premier League for a massive club like Manchester City, though, and we did well enough after a shaky start. My first game resulted in creating a goal for David White, who rounded off Niall Quinn's shot at goal, only for us to be thwarted by Andy Sinton who, buoyed no doubt by his England selection, had the confidence to try a long-range shot which flew into the top corner past TC. It unfortunately took me a long time to register my first goal for the club, and I wasn't being blessed with much luck. We lost away at Blackburn when we dominated the game. Things such as the utter skinning of David May at right-back, and landing the ball on Quinny's head, who then produced the perfect execution only for it to bounce up and over the bar were happening. Away at Middlesbrough, I hit the post from a header, with the 'keeper completely beaten. The ball fell to a defender, not to one of our attackers, and this was indicative of the start we were having. Quinny then got sent off and we left Ayresome Park empty-handed. We eventually beat Norwich at home 3–1, and this settled us down. We had a good FA Cup run, reaching the quarter-finals at home to Spurs, and I felt sure we were going to do something special in this competition. It was another false dawn, however. Again I had picked out a striker, Mike Sheron, and we went one up. Suddenly we capitulated, losing four quick goals, although Terry Phelan scored one for us to give the score some respect. This sparked a fan riot of the bad old days of the seventies, which included a full pitch invasion and mounted police on the field of play. I can remember seeing one horse crap right by the side of the touch line and thinking to myself that it was a good job well done. Spurs had become our bogey side this season – they had also beaten us in the League Cup, again after we had contrived to miss chance after chance. The season which had promised so much just petered out with a humiliating 5–2 home defeat by Everton, which summed us up.

Another summer in the hospitals of the North West and a few exams was all I had to look forward to, and I really couldn't wait to get back to Maine Road to get the job done properly this time. This year, the pre-season tour was to Ireland and Holland and looked interesting. City liked to go on trips. In April 1993, just after my first son, William, was born, we were dragged off to Japan to play a couple of J League teams. Talk about a long way to go for a friendly. But there must have been some money in it for City, or it is unlikely we would have gone. Nippon is a weird place, and from what I could glean after our small visit their national pastimes seemed to be eating raw fish, hitting golf balls across sky scrapers and getting pissed after work. (Seems like a great place.) It was another experience, though, and we battled out two more scoreless draws against superior South American opposition, which seemed to be the composition of these new J League sides. We also played Torino out in Japan and were getting the right run around. At half-time I said, 'Gaffer, why don't we take our own ball out second half because at least that way we might get a kick?' Reidy, as quick as a flash, retorted with, 'F\*\*k that! They'll probably take that off us as well.'

There was tension around Maine Road when we returned to the throng. There were rumours that Peter Reid and Sam Ellis were under pressure to succeed and that they had better try to get some results early on or they would be for the high jump. This was outrageous as the club had finished fifth, fifth and eighth in the top flight during the previous three seasons. These lads had done tremendously well at City and, given time, would achieve even greater things. But the powers that be panicked and got greedier, and didn't City suffer in the ensuing years? When we were in Holland and Ireland there were some incidents, such as the delaying of an aircraft, which didn't help confidence, but nothing very serious went on and certainly nothing that warranted the witch hunt that happened against the gaffer and Sam. I felt that these two were dedicated men and so were the players. Generally, we all wanted to succeed for Manchester City, and I believe that in time we would have been a very useful outfit indeed, winning something in due course. The gaffer made a couple of new signings, namely a Dutch lad called Alfons Groenendijk, whom they were eulogising about at great lengths regarding his left foot. I knew that it was designed to wind me up, as Sam had worked me out to be a player who gave the impression of not caring but actually did, deep down. It was funny really because I took one look at him and knew instantly that he was too fragile for the Premiership, but I went along with the laugh. He and another Dutch lad called Michel Vonk couldn't hack the mental or lunatic side to English football, which was evident when we used to play corridor cricket and whack the tennis ball into the room in which they were resting. They used to lose their rag in tandem. The Dutch don't really appreciate cricket. They have a team in the knock-out every year and a one-day World Cup team, but cricket in hotel corridors is not their cup of tea.

The first game of the season was against Leeds United at home. I was placed on the right side of midfield to make way for my Dutch counterpart on the left. We huffed and puffed for 80 minutes until finally I was switched to my proper wing, at which point we took the lead. I can remember that I was greeted with an ironic cheer when I ran over to the left wing and an even bigger cheer when I created the room for our opening goal. Then, in true fashion, we let them equalise from a corner in the dying seconds. This was a tragedy and spelled the beginning of the end for Reidy and Sam and consequently myself.

A most weird thing occurred that I hadn't heard of before or subsequently. The chairman, Peter Swales, had employed an ex-journalist called John Maddocks, who must have been a friend or he must have had something on Swales. From what I could gather he was a cross between a liaison officer for Swales and the management and a mole, only his literal presence was actually larger than his metaphorical one, so more hippo really. He used to skulk around the club, passing asides and messages on, but no one really knew what he was doing. One day, just before the management was sacked, Sam came up to me after a game, put his arm around me and said, 'Well done, but Maddocks didn't want you to play today.' I was naturally flabbergasted. Maddocks shouldn't have had any say in who was selected. Who did he think he was, having the audacity to give orders to the club like that, having the nerve to tell them their job? It must have come from above, I thought, or did it? Like true men, Reid and Sam obviously told him where to get off and I played. Not long after that the two men were given their marching orders. I felt sick about this. It's always difficult when people who believed in you are given the boot. It isolates you and leaves you vulnerable for when the next bloke comes in. You often feel that you've let them down, too, and I certainly thought that I had done that. Since I had been at City, I had not played consistently at my best. I had my moments but I had not put a run of form together that I knew I was capable of, even though I had felt that this was just around the corner, and sure enough it was.

Peter Reid and Sam Ellis were sacked after just four games of the new season. It had to be politics. Some said that the chairman wanted rid of Sam and to keep Reidy on his own, but footballers have in general more honour than members of boards and so Reid was never going accept this. To be fair, these two are shrewd men and didn't panic. They knew that good things would come to them again if they waited long enough and this proved true, as they are still in good jobs in football and doing well. We all waited for the next move. Lots of big names were being bandied about, the favourite being Joe Royle. This was very exciting for me, the prospect of my old mate joining this club, but it was not to be. He had destiny laid out for him at Everton. It was a real shame because he would have been useful later in the process of rescuing City from the edge of oblivion in 1999–2000. The day of reckoning arrived and we were to be introduced to our new gaffer before the home tie with Coventry City, for which game Tony Book was put in charge. The announcement was made: 'Here he is, boys, the new manager – Brian Horton!' The pin dropped like an iron bar on sheet metal, closely followed by my jaw and everyone else's. 'Brian Who?' we all thought. I had heard of him, but most of the lads hadn't and I can see that it came as a bit of a shock to them. He had been manager of Oxford beforehand and had done reasonably well with them. Quite where the idea comes from that if you can steer a low division ship that you will automatically be able to steer a high-flying ship comes from I don't know. Similarly, if you've played at the highest level, it is expected that you have some notion of how to run a club of any size. It is, I'm afraid, the luck of the draw if you're gambling on someone without a track record in that particular field.

Following the game against Coventry our new gaffer came in to tell us how pleased he was with the performance and said that we had worked very hard indeed. I tried my hardest to make an impression in the side and worked hard in training as well, but things didn't work out. I was suddenly dropped after we had made a brief visit to Turkey to play Besiktas in a friendly on yet another quick jaunt. Again it was the dark conspirator on the inside who was trying his hand at team selection and squad cleansing. An away game at Sheffield United wasn't the best of days and wasn't the best of grounds for me. That morning we had been going through the set pieces on the training ground. Note the similarity in preparation to when I was at Watford, with this same-day set-piece rubbish. It shows a complete lack of confidence in the lads. You could say who can blame them, but on the other hand there are ways of fine-tuning defensive strategy without the need to drag the lads in on the morning of a game. While doing 'defending corners' the gaffer had said, 'Who is going to pick Adrian Littlejohn up at corners? He's dangerous,' or words to that effect. Before anyone could react I chipped in with, 'Never mind Littlejohn, it's Robin Hood and Friar Tuck that you want to be worried about!'

Now this went down like a lead balloon with the gaffer and his assistant, Dave Moss, who must have had a sense of humour short circuit and obviously couldn't see the funny side of it. Much laughter from the other chaps only compounded the reaction, and I was asked to leave the training area. Fair enough, no big issue was made of it. We threw away a one-goal advantage and scraped a draw, which didn't go down well, but at least none of the characters of Sherwood Forest scored and the goal was in open play too. We were given a bollocking and asked to come in for some meaningless training the following day. Shortly after this game we played Oldham at Maine Road, and midway through the second half, after a maze-like run and a shot which hit the post, I was substituted. I felt that this was done to try to humiliate me in front of ex-players, fans and, of course, management. I could be paranoid and totally wrong, but there is a good chance that this is what happened as I was playing well and I know how these amateur psychologists work. Several days later, on a Thursday morning, I was summoned to the manager's office, where Moss and Maddocks were in attendance. I was told that I was really superfluous to requirements but that they couldn't force me out as I still had 33 months left on my contract; however, they said that Joe Royle had been in for me and that I should really go up to Boundary Park to chat to him, otherwise I would find myself playing at Barrow that very evening for City's stiffs. So what was it, Barrow tonight or wheelbarrow for my cash tomorrow? It wasn't an easy decision to make, because I knew that Oldham's reign in the Premier League was tenuous, and a loss of this status would mean a loss of status for me. City, on the other hand, were fairly safe at the time of asking; however, I also knew that if this lot remained in charge then my life would be made miserable and that City would fall into the abyss anyway. I decided to rid myself of my shackles and return home. On the short journey to Boundary Park I had time for reflection and reverie about the last 15 months. It was now October, the nights were drawing in early and car headlights were beginning to come on as I joined the madhouse of the M62. Quite simply, I'd underachieved and, like the Watford experience, I could blame any number of individuals and circumstances. Yet again it fell squarely upon my shoulders, as right now I was the only person in the world thinking about this problem. No one else was giving it a second thought, and I suppose that this is the way in professional football. You've just got to get on with things, though, and that is what I was going to do. I cast my mind back to that first journey through the Dolomites with my City fan companion. I could well have been tied to a radiator in the Lebanon during the last 15 months and what difference would it have made? City was life at the very top and I had some great experiences, such as the Manchester derby games and the trips to foreign lands, and though I feel I wasn't a great success it was a life-changing experience and one that I shall always be grateful for.

As I mentioned there were a couple of lads that I was a bit suspicious of when I first joined City, and this is always the case with football or indeed, I suspect, with any team sport. You just don't get total squad harmony and perhaps that's a good thing. Fitzroy Simpson and I didn't exactly hit it off at first, though I am glad to say that we are good mates now and I loved playing in the Masters with him on Sky Sports. He was very energetic and tough, and I accused him of throwing his weight around in training a little bit too vigorously and things got tense. We were on a night out in Manchester and drinks were flowing. Mike Milligan joined the fray (which is always dangerous) and we were in an Irish pub (another mistake). All was calm. I can remember having a little disagreement with Fitz over footy: he loves the game and enjoys a philosophical chat, and as proceedings drifted I could see him getting more exasperated. I caught him sitting down in the corner in a very vulnerable spot as I was standing at the bar with Sam Ellis and Mike Milligan. Tony Coton had just rugby-tackled his fifth women to the floor (his little party piece in which he would just pounce on a passing woman en route to the toilet, cushion her perfectly to the deck and then right her and release her as if nothing out of the ordinary had happened) when I seized my opportunity amid the commotion that TC had caused. I picked up one of those plastic Strongbow Cider drip trays off the bar, which had a triangular shape to give the arrowhead effect, and flung it on top of one of the rotating fans that dangled from the ceiling. The shot was perfect and it landed smack on top of the huge rotating wooden blades creating a shearing and splintering sound that deafened the pub. The lights flashed and the fans ground to a halt, and everyone stopped to try to work out what had happened as nobody had seen me do it. Then Sam said, 'Who the f**k did that?' Fitzroy staggered to the bar with a large plastic splinter about 12 inches long sticking out of his forehead, blood running down his face. Sam swung round on his chair and asked me. I immediately blamed Milly. To this day Fitz, Sam and everyone else think it was Milligan, who nobly took the rap for me. They wouldn't have a go at him. I know it was childish and dangerous, but it was funny.

# six

## Never Return
## [Barrow or Wheelbarrow]

They do say in football that it is often a mistake to return to a former club, especially one where you have had some success. This is because you will never, in the eyes of the fans or the media, recapture the glory days with which you'll obviously be compared. I must admit I did have my reservations about going back to Boundary Park, and not just through looking in the paper at their dodgy League position. The previous Christmas I had been invited back to the town to switch on the Yuletide lights. Some clerk to the Mayor announced, 'And here he is: Rick Holden to switch on the lights.' I stepped forward onto the balcony and was greeted with a resounding chorus of boos and hisses. Bloody charming, I thought. The mayor and his entourage, obviously viewing it as a mistake, quickly vanished from the scene, leaving me to ignominiously pick my way through the town hall and slip away into the night. Before leaving I thanked the Oldham public for their traditional warm Lancastrian welcome over the microphone, which didn't go down too well either. My misgivings about returning to the town may have been justified, but I consoled myself that they were probably the same fans that I called morons a couple of years earlier. I decided to go for it. I would still be playing Premier League football, after all, and that wasn't bad. I had a real sense of purpose about my return in that I wanted to preserve Oldham's top-flight status, which I had previously spent three years in helping to achieve. Should you go with someone whom you love, but doesn't love you, or with someone who loves you, but whom you may not love? It's a tricky one.

I was greeted warmly enough by the lads at the club, and the staff were their usual open selves. The atmosphere in the changing room was similar, if a little subdued, and the only noticeable thing that had changed on the team coach journeys was Norland replacing Marshy in the Hearts school and Neil Pointon's obsession with war videos, which he played at full volume. That bloke ruined most of the hit films of the late eighties and early nineties for me. It is impossible to say whether I have seen a film or not because of this subliminal noise invasion that I had to endure and all the unavoidable momentary glances at the screen on the long-distance bus rides. Imagine that you are about to play an important card and there's a huge explosion behind you some three feet away on the telly, followed by 10 rounds of machine-gun fire, and you get the picture.

We were not the side we used to be, but there was tremendous fighting spirit, as they had proved the season before when avoiding relegation by the skin of their teeth and simultaneously wrecking Aston Villa's chance of winning the League title. Personally, I had never felt better and was like a coiled spring waiting to be let free. This happened in my return home debut against Arsenal. I was giving Lee Dixon more than just a roasting, in fact he was getting the full Yorkshire and sprouts treatment on top. How we hadn't scored was down mainly to Seaman in goal and a slice of luck, which wasn't forthcoming. Just after the half-hour mark I raced to the edge of the pitch in chase of a wayward pass and collided into a 50–50 challenge with Dixon. As I struggled to get up he did something to prevent me from doing so and at the same time threw the ball away. I walked over to him and pushed him in his chest with both hands, to which he responded with a full Klinsmann backwards dive to the ground. It looked like he'd been floored by a bomb. It was like that Di Canio incident when he pushed the ref over. I did not for one minute expect the reaction I got from Dixon and was even more amazed when the referee ran over brandishing his notebook and issued a red card for me and a yellow for the England full-back. I know that I'm a big strong lad and definitely not the conventional build for a winger, but this was ridiculous. A red card for pushing someone who then made a huge meal of it – he had to be joking. Joe did say in the press that he would have to keep me off the weights during the week, though. Ironically, Lee is now a TV pundit and offers his opinions on things such as players diving and not being honest.

My only professional dismissal was caused by me being too pumped up for the game, the overreaction of a player and a renowned referee with a penchant for controversy. My only other sending-offs have been in two games on the Isle of Man and one while playing for my college back in 1984 in a game at Newcastle. What a showing-up, though. *Match of the Day* re-ran it and over played it, and so did Sky TV. Unfortunately we didn't win the game as we should have, after clearly dominating it, and the two dropped points were vital at the end of the season. This little cameo put me out of the frame for three games, during which time we failed to collect any points. This meant that I had to try to help kickstart the momentum again, and I feared that the impact of my arrival might not have had the same effect as it might have done had I been able to play in all the games. We did quite well, though, and rolled Chelsea over at Stamford Bridge, which gave me great pleasure. It is not that I have anything in particular against Chelsea, it was just that the chairman of the club was a little condescending in the match programme, and I think that we all enjoyed ramming his words down his big gob.

We began to slowly pick up points and edge out of danger, but then something peculiar happened which, when I trace everything back, was our ultimate downfall. We faced Derby County in the FA Cup. They were in the division below us, but nevertheless were a strong outfit. In a titanic struggle, in which I scored, we overcame them and the dream was suddenly alive once again. Four years previously, when we were upstarts on plastic from the Second Division, we became household names and everyone's favourite second team due to our tremendous Cup exploits, and it looked like that might happen again. What days they had been. Those days were the best of my sporting life. Reflecting back to 1989–90, everything we touched had turned to gold, and we became a footballing David slaying Goliaths from all around. The League Cup, at the time known as the Littlewoods Cup, was where it all began in a 7–0 thrashing of poor Scarborough. It's quite funny because someone from their camp expressed disappointment at only being drawn against Oldham as a reward for battling their way through the initial two-match home and away series involving all the lower division outfits and then taking the scalp of Chelsea. They got truly spanked and Frank Bunn made history by scoring six of the goals. The other one, and the pick of the bunch, was by Andy Ritchie. I did feel a little sorry for them, and knew what they meant with their deflated reaction to the draw. Our crowds were low at the time, so there wasn't even the consolation of a big purse for them for the bout.

Previously, we had dealt with Leeds United in two thrilling games and then Arsenal, the League champions, who were dispatched with consummate ease 3–1. I will never forget the look of bewilderment on George Graham's face during the game and Kevin Richardson's kind words afterwards. It was becoming a roller-coaster ride of fantasy proportions and everyone in the town was becoming caught up in it. Football does this like nothing else I know, and some people have even produced figures to prove statistically that production goes up in manufacturing industries in towns where the football club is successful. It has something to do with the feel-good factor. I walked around my tiny village of Springhead and all the shops, the butchers, bakers and even the candlestick maker had Oldham paraphernalia such as scarves, team pictures and cut-out imitations of the League Cup displayed in the windows. Everywhere you went people would stop you and chat about the latest epic encounter, and to make matters worse I had my name on the side of my car. I was sponsored by a firm known as Oldham Motor Bodies who, in exchange for an annual respray, were associated with our success at Latics.

Next to feel the heat were Southampton, whom we'd drawn away in the quarter-finals, and it was on paper a tricky fixture. This seemed to be the case when, following a dubious penalty, we looked like we were on the verge of extinction. Luckily, with one last surge of energy, I managed to skid a cross in behind the Saints' defence, and there was Andy Ritchie on hand to break their hearts. We thus forced a replay up at Boundary Park and duly powered past them into the semi-finals 2–0. More fever pitch in town, which was highlighted by the queues along

Sheepfoot Lane which stretched as far as the eye could see as excited punters gathered to try to secure semi-final tickets. We had been drawn against fellow Second Division opponents West Ham. Although they had done well in reaching this stage, they were having a bit of a torrid time under Lou Macari and we took advantage of this in the home first leg. In front of a capacity crowd of 19,000 we mutilated the Hammers 6–0. Poor Lou got the sack after this, but it wasn't his fault. I felt afterwards that nobody would have stopped us on that evening, and it was probably the most emphatic and ruthless display in soccer in the last 10 years. Twenty years since it happened, I don't think there has been such a mauling as this since in such a big game, although it would have been double figures but for an ageing Phil Parks in goal, as he pulled off three or four superb stops. With the tie effectively over, Billy Bonds, that Hammers legend, had the task of trying to restore pride. We were in a strange and unfamiliar position of damage limitation, and Joe took steps to avoid a catastrophe by naming Andy Rhodes as the second substitute, just in case the first-choice 'keeper, captain Jon Hallworth, was injured early on. These were the days before three subs, or three from five as it is now. In the end we lost 3–0, which we weren't best pleased with, but then again we had done it and become the first-ever Oldham team to reach a Wembley Final. Things were now in a frenzied state back in Oldham, and I thought things must surely settle down for a couple of months before the Final.

I had not reckoned on the power of the FA Cup, however, which we were also heavily involved in. If I thought that the Littlewoods Cup fired the imagination, the FA Cup metaphorically explodes it. The massive struggle against Everton's aggressive and grumpy ex-champions was fairytale stuff. We went 2–0 behind at home, but then forced a replay at Goodison Park. At Goodison we took the lead in extra-time, only to be denied by a late penalty. In the second replay, we won with Marshy's famous penalty and even more infamous celebration. Graham Taylor's Aston Villa then visited the Ice Station and, to his utter amazement, he watched his side, packed with internationals like David Platt, get put to the sword 3–0 while hardly creating a chance. This put the region at an even higher level of excitement and the buzz around the place increased rather than calmed down.

What next? The semi-final draw was between Crystal Palace, Liverpool, Manchester United and ourselves. We came out against United and were scheduled to play in the afternoon following Liverpool and Palace. The excitement of facing Manchester United in an FA Cup semi-final was out of this world. They were struggling at the time, and Alex Ferguson was reportedly under pressure to provide a trophy. The last thing Sir Alex, as he is now, wanted was this loose cannon called Oldham Athletic. The Sunday morning game was an absolute cracker in which Palace came from behind to unhinge Liverpool's famed defence from set pieces to win 4–3. How could our game live up to this?

After a see-sawing contest the game was locked at 3–3 after 89 minutes. Then came one of the defining moments of my career and, for that matter, I believe in the career of Sir Alex. With everyone looking at the ref and waiting for him to blow for full-time, I managed to get the ball out wide on the left. Instead of heading for the by-line, I cut inside and hit it with my swinger (right foot to the uninitiated). I thought, 'It's in. It has to be.' Jim 'no teeth' Leighton was well beaten as he made a desperate dive to his right, but the ball glanced the outside of the post and went for a goal-kick. That would have been it. No comebacks from that. The whistle went and a replay followed at the same venue, Maine Road. If that shot had gone in then, though, what of Manchester United? What even of Sir Alex, what of us? Cruelly, at 1–1 in the replay, I was caught out of position, allowing my opposing full-back, Mike Phelan from Colne, to race through to tee up Mark Robins to score the winner. What a bummer. It was made worse by the waving away of a goal by Nick Henry which everyone believed was over the line. The pictures tell it all. That is the magic of the Cup, though. The excitement and expectation, and the despair. Nothing can prepare you for the ultimate disaster and, to be honest, no one ever talks about it beforehand. We had set the competition on fire and were quite literally the thickness of the goal posts from a second Wembley visit. This would have been unique for any club, let alone a Second Division one as unfashionable as Oldham.

Such was the nationwide interest that I even appeared on the television sports quiz show *Question of Sport* in Bill Beaumont's team. The magic then drained away, however, and the defeat at the hands of United affected the rest of the season. We slipped to eighth place in the League. More bad luck and Forest and Cloughie knew it. A rebounded effort turned Nigel Jemson into an instant hero for Forest. Maybe it is sour grapes but we didn't deserve that outcome. Again a competition that we had set alight provided us in the end with only sad memories on the final day. At the hotel reception somewhere in Northamptonshire we nearly lost control and thankfully the pain of defeat didn't turn out worse. I have since learned never to plan a reception for supposed celebration after a Cup Final. It's best to let the post-match things take care of themselves – after all, these are nearly always the best nights.

You can imagine my alarm, then, in early 1994 when I began to detect the same thing happening again in the FA Cup. This was accepted by the Oldham faithful as a respite from the dogged relegation battle we were embroiled in, and although we were not quite pitted against the same quality of opposition as in the 1990 campaign, the excitement level was still there. Cup runs are great for League form at first in that it gives you extra confidence to take to the League, but when it goes wrong, it goes very wrong. I just knew it, and again it comes down to luck. We drew Bolton Wanderers in the quarter-final at Burnden Park. I was to come up against my old mate, Mr Brown, and the papers made a bit of a thing about it. Unfortunately I had taken a hell of a whack at Goodison the week before on my calf muscle and it was very sore indeed. I had physio on it three times a day, and though it wasn't 100 per cent, it was good enough for me to be a distraction policy. A bad mistake by the Bolton defence let in Darren Beckford and he made no mistake with the finish. Our 1–0 victory saw us come up once again against Manchester United. Before this semi-final, we pulled out a couple of great results by hammering QPR 4–1 and turning Chelsea over 2–1. This was my favourite ever League game – I had never played better and completely ran them ragged. I did feel we were going to make it and escape the horror of the drop after these performances, but then again here was the irony of the FA Cup. Arsenal and Spurs had set about destroying the magic of Wembley by playing an FA Cup semi-final on the hallowed turf some three years earlier in 1991 and now, controversially, we were to do the same. The other semi was also played there between Luton and Chelsea, two teams that we would have had a great chance against, but oh no, we had to draw Manchester again.

We set our stall out to stop them cutting us up on the break with all their pace, which is what they had done to us so many times in the past. They had handed out some big defeats to us, like 5–2 and 6–3, when we had played them in the League, which proved that we could score against them, but so often they would sweep out of their own defence with Giggs and Kanchelskis, and before you knew what was happening we would be taking a kick off. And it worked too. We frustrated them beyond belief and created our fair share of chances, but couldn't force home a goal. The game went to extra-time, and from my corner the film maniac Neil Pointon rammed the ball home. This had to be it. We were now seconds from the end – could we hang on?

I raced down the wing and took the challenge to my old mate Dennis Irwin. He fouled me, and as the ref awarded the free kick and Dennis switched off, I quickly played the ball into Graeme Sharpe's path, and with only Schmeichel to beat he hit it into the side netting. What should have been 2–0 was left perilously at 1–0. Then another career defining moment for me and Sir Alex occurred. We had possession of the ball, and all Neil Pointon had to do was to give it to me and I would have set off down the wing on another lung burster. He panicked and hoofed it into the crowd. The Red Devils got the ball, slung it into the box, and after an appeal for off-side it landed on the famous boot of Mark Hughes, who let rip his trademark volley into the back of the net. That was it. There would be no second chance. After the game I drowned myself in the bath. The image of that goal stayed with me for a long time. I knew that it would be catastrophic and I think it had a depressing effect on the nation as a whole, apart from United fans. The replay at Maine Road was a disaster, and although Neil scored another goal we were blown away.

It could have been so different, and it should have been. Our relegation struggle involved Spurs, Everton and Sheffield United, and our next home game was due to be against Spurs on the same night as the replay. If we had won at Wembley I feel sure that we would have swept Tottenham aside, but that game was put back and when we did come to play them we were a depressed shadow of ourselves, and we slumped to defeat. In fact, we didn't win another game that season, and on the last

Saturday of the season we quietly slipped out of the Premier League, hopefully not forever, but it felt like it at the time.

Something strange happened during the last game of the season up at Everton, who were entertaining the Wombles of Wimbledon. The Wombles sped into a three-goal lead thanks to goals from Orinoco, Tobermory and Great Uncle Bulgaria, only to let it slip and allow Everton to escape relegation with a last-minute 4–3 victory. Had we won at Norwich and Everton lost, we would have stayed up but we drew 1–1; however, the goalie for Wimbledon was none other than Hans Segers, who later on was to become embroiled, along with John Fashanu and Bruce Grobbelaar, in a betting scandal over alleged match-fixing. I'm not for one minute saying that the Dons threw their game up at Everton, but it gets you thinking, and with the sort of luck we were having it wouldn't have been beyond the realms of fantasy if they had. Dejected, we headed back up north and I pondered on my loss of Premier League status. I should have gone into Joe's office and asked for my name to be circulated for transfer, but I'm not that kind of person and I put trying to restore Oldham's pride and position before my own career. Although this appears on the face of it completely stupid, I felt it was my duty to stay and support Joe and Willy as they had supported me. I retired back to Embsay to ponder on the season and to play some cricket.

Embsay had a great season at cricket and we swept all before us. I was bowling at my fastest and most aggressive and thoroughly enjoyed it. When I returned to Oldham I felt refreshed and ready for the challenge of trying to bounce straight back into the Premier. We started well, hammering Charlton 5–2 on the opening day, and were soon back at the top of the League. It would, I can state in all confidence, have been a walk back to the top flight if circumstances hadn't changed. I remember the shock of it all as if it was only yesterday, and the disappointment is still acute now some 15 years later.

I rate Joe Royle, as much as a thinker as anything else, and rarely does he make an error in judgement. Only twice can I say that he got it slightly wrong, and unfortunately this decision was close to his worst. Prior to his departure, he had recommended current player Graeme Sharpe as his replacement, not the least because he was sitting on a big contract, and for that money he might as well earn his coin. It was a gamble and could have come off, and Sharpe may well have been the next in a long line of great Scottish managers. It didn't, though, and everyone suffered for it, especially me. Joe's last game in charge was away at Arsenal in the Littlewoods Cup, in which we were turned over. I had started the season quite well and then found myself on the bench on the odd occasion. It didn't matter that much as I was always thrown on later and looked at it as a bit of a rest. I had been inches from knocking Arsenal out of the Cup in the original tie at Boundary Park when I came on as a sub, but found myself picking splinters out of my arse on the bench for the replay. I didn't know at the time that it was my last game under Joe for Oldham and that it was the beginning of the end for me at the Latics. We lost 2–0 and got a bit of a bollocking, and it probably helped the gaffer to make up his mind about joining Everton. On the Thursday we had a meeting in which Joe and Willy let us know of their intentions. They wished us all the best and then left. I was sad on this day and even more gutted when I found out the ultimate outcome. The side had already been picked by Joe for Saturday's game against Luton at home, and I was down to play. We tried hard but couldn't break them down, and so it ended goalless. Sharpe's first game in charge at West Brom was very enlightening. We all travelled down and he named the side in the changing rooms. He then named the subs. He said nothing more. I was just left standing there. He completely ignored me, and so I left the changing rooms. We got stuffed 3–1 and were embarrassing, and I enjoyed watching the new manager fumble his way through his first game.

On the Monday during training I overheard Sharpe talking to Mark Brennan, who had replaced me on the left, saying words to the effect that he was going to have to go for it so was playing me on the wing because we needed some crosses. I never spoke to him, but we recorded three consecutive wins and I had done most of the damage. Andy Ritchie scored a great hat-trick against Port Vale at Boundary Park with a little assistance from his old left-wing buddy. I felt sure that I had proved a point and that even if Sharpe didn't particularly want to play me that common sense would prevail. I don't really know why he took a dislike to me. Could it have been the shit-throwing incident? Or was it because he thought me a threat? Perhaps he just didn't rate me and fancied his own kind of player. Management does funny things to some people and they become almost obsessed by their new club. It is a case of 'this club is now mine, and I'll have my own players that I can control and my own staff that I can trust, and then I will succeed'. But they always forget one thing and that's results. It doesn't matter if you don't get on with a lad if they can do the business. It's even better that way as you will be getting something from him that you wouldn't ordinarily expect. Too often you can pick up the papers and read about a fall out between a player and manager, and this then affects the professional relationship. This should never happen and can be put down to lack of man-management skills in most cases. As I write there will be scores of players up and down the country in professional football who are training on their own or with the kids because he's had a fall out with the gaffer and has been banished for being a naughty boy. If it wasn't so pathetic it would be hilarious. I suffered this ignominy at Watford, but to his credit Graeme Sharpe didn't stoop to that level. The reason that they do this is because the manager thinks that if he allows the player to train with the rest of the first-team squad, he will be a disruptive influence. This is schoolboy psychology stuff that wouldn't be out of place in a playground.

From that day in December 1994 against Port Vale I never started another game for Oldham, although Sharpe used me as a sub on a few occasions. I hated this time. Before a match he would name the side and I would be left out or on the bench. After 14 March 1995 I never featured again, but always had to be there. I would sit and watch the games as our lads edged through the rest of the season to finish 14th in the League, and I'd be thinking, 'Am I reduced to this?' I predicted a sad ending to Sharpe's plight and I wasn't wrong. I hadn't predicted a sad end for me though.

Summer 1995, and I again returned to the cricket field for some sanctuary and thoroughly enjoyed the experience. Embsay continued to dominate the local scene, and I was bowling with quite a degree of venom. I was excited at the prospect of a new club and was hoping that one would come in for me. I hadn't got my megaphone out and advertised that I was a free agent, or as good as, and perhaps this was why there was no movement. At 31 years old I felt I still had a lot to offer, but Oldham weren't interested. I had got to the forgotten man or leper stage in the club now in that I was training on my own or with the reserve-team coach, Andy Holden, and occasionally with Andy Ritchie who, although exiled to Scarborough, was permitted to train at the club. Graeme Sharpe's regime was destined for failure by now – you cannot exile your best players at a small club like Oldham and get away with it, because there are just not the resources to replace them. It was all rather sad and predictable, but I had to move on regardless of my affection for the place. The person they had entrusted to run the club had no time or sentiment for me, so what did I care now? I had made a big impact on the club and would remain forever in the memories and history books of Oldham, so balls to them. It was time to go.

I have to mention one thing before I shut the Oldham experience down. The game is littered with players who should have played for England but didn't, some because of personality clashes or some because they were just completely overlooked. Andy Ritchie is just such a player. How on earth he was never given a chance to play for England is mind-boggling. There was not a better player in the British game than Andy between 1988 and 1994. His all-encompassing game of touch, passing and vision was supreme, not to mention his great goals, and his being ignored just sums up the people in charge of the national side at the time. As for Oldham, they are in my heart but it makes me weep at times when I look at it all now, and I could have changed it around in 10 minutes if I was allowed to bring the old guard and the old spirit back in.

# seven

## Illumination

When Joe Royle decided that enough was enough at Oldham and took the deserved gambit of returning to his roots at Everton I was disappointed, but I vowed that I would try to make the most of it without him. It may seem a strange thing to say on the face of it, but I'd only really played with full gusto for a happy club and Oldham with JR was certainly always that. I loved to play with a smile on my face and with a happy heart, and when a club became turgid, dour and downright mean and insensitive I just switched off. Most players, if they're honest, will tell you the same. The club is an inanimate object, often owned by a tycoon, sometimes with a hard business edge, which fans somehow take to their soul. Yet the real lifeblood, zest and character is set by the management and playing staff. At Oldham, we had glorious management staff who bought players who were characters, who would respond to their management style and who would act out on the pitch the fantasies and beliefs of the management. In short, Joe was the creator of the modern Oldham and unfortunately, as with many an empire, when he left, the ship became rudderless, cast adrift and ready for the vandals to descend.

I stayed in the hope that we would get a big name, a large character to impose himself on the club. I should have known better. I should have learned from the Manchester City experience when they sacked Reidy, a real heart and soul man, that I'd be disappointed. Sometimes, quite often in fact, club chairmen react hastily by sacking a manager and then they panic to get someone new in and, in effect, do the equivalent of sacking Franz Klammer as the skiing instructor and replacing him with Eddie the Eagle. Oldham were no different and they did things on the cheap by appointing Graeme Sharpe as manager because he was still contracted to the club for two years and therefore making him player/manager was an inexpensive and easy option – two jobs for the price of one. I knew that the writing was on the wall when, after scoring two goals in the game prior to Joe leaving, I was promptly dropped for Sharpe's first game in charge. Team morale was as low as a snake's wedding tackle. Sharpy was a popular member of the squad when he was a player – I certainly liked him – but I just thought it was the wrong appointment. Training was suddenly different. Willie's running-based training, particularly in pre-season, was met with raised eyebrows by Graeme because it was different at Everton, where they had success at national and international level off the back of a special Howard Kendall/Colin Harvey five-a-side based style with the occasional 400-metre run thrown in. To be fair, Sharpe always claimed to have a bad back and did work hard, especially in matches, and proved to be a very good leader of the line. He was not the fans' favourite, however, and his appointment was met with a 'let's give him a chance' attitude around the borough of Oldham. The fans' true favourite, Andy Ritchie, was completely overlooked, and he was subsequently exiled to Scarborough for a couple of years by the new emperor.

I didn't really understand why I was rejected by Sharpe. Some players said it was because he thought me to be a disruptive character who harboured too many dangerous opinions, or it could have been revenge for the infamous lift incident in Sweden a couple of years earlier. Either way, I found myself as popular as a swarm of wasps in a beer garden, and, at the very best, I was on the bench but normally reduced to playing reserve-team football at far-flung grounds around northern England when I should have been at home or down the pub, wasps and all, in the beer garden. I did not even have the pleasure of playing on Boundary Park in front of the Latics' faithful, as for some strange reason the stiffs were now entertaining the footballing populus at Stalybridge on a Tuesday or a Wednesday evening, yet another impossible northern town to get to from anywhere, let alone Skipton. It must have been a decision by the management in order to try to preserve the

Oldham playing surface for first-team football. It worked – you should have seen the opposition knock the ball around on a Saturday afternoon. All in all, it was a nightmare of hideous proportions and I had to get out and get out quickly. It was slowly destroying me, even though I tried to just think of the money.

I have little sympathy for modern-day Premier League clubs who bleat about so-called loyalty from top players, demonstrated by Paolo Di Canio, Pierre Van Hooijdonk, Stan Collymore, Nicholas Anelka and Jimmy Floyd Hasselbaink. Thanks to the inspirational Jean-Marc Bosman, these men have exercised their rights to freedom of employment, which is the norm in most other businesses in the world. For years British clubs have made players rot in the reserves when out of favour, forcing them to ask for transfers and subsequently forfeiting money rightly owed to them from transfer fees. Alternatively, they would simply let them die out of contract and cast rumours about the player's reliability to any future employer. Players are now turning the tables on the club hierarchies that have been allowed to get away with their schoolyard bully-boy tactics. Why did club owners allow their managers to get away with this sort of behaviour? Why, for example, didn't Ian Stott, the Oldham chairman, approach Graeme Sharpe and ask him what the bloody hell he was playing at, leaving Rick Holden, the proven leading goal maker of the last five or six years (in all divisions of football, including the Premiership) out of the team in second-class football? I doubt it was personal, but I could be wrong.

I do know one reason why he preferred Mark Brennan to me, and that was because he saw a different sort of player in Mark. A man of considerable weight and influence in Everton's halcyon days was Kevin Sheedy, generally acknowledged as having one of the sweetest left pegs in the modern game. He operated as a mid-fielder, playing more on the inside than on the wing, and his trademark was a very accurate diagonal ball deep into the box for Sharpe or Andy Gray to attack at the back stick. This was precisely the position and style of play that Mark Brennan adopted and was very good at. This is a very effective way of playing left wing, or left-hand-side midfield as it is referred to today. This form of play is essentially a defensive tactic designed to make a team very hard to break down.

The strategy basically consisted of a back eight protecting the goalkeeper, and in front of all of this were two very clever aggressive centre-forwards who could score goals almost out of nothing. Anyone who could score the number of goals Sharpe and Gray did for Everton deserved more than the odd medal they received with this approach. Incidentally, Everton had an exceptional back four and a world-class (if a little odd) goalkeeper, so no wonder they were virtually unbeatable at times.

The style I have just described sets out to win every game 1–0, and more often than not it works; certainly it is unlikely to concede more than the odd goal a game. The kind of approach used by Evertonian old-boy Joe Royle was the total opposite in that he employed an attacking style with two attacking wingers. Midfielders and defenders also ran all over the place. The philosophy, whether he liked it or not, was win, and win by enjoying yourself with free entertaining play. Consequently, we would win or lose by the odd goal in seven and damn good fun it was too. In order to score this number of goals you had to create chance after chance, and the best way to achieve this was to supply crosses continually, not from deep with huge diagonals, but from the by-line, the old-fashioned way. The ball is pulled back so the centre-forward is running onto the ball. In order to achieve this, one ingredient is essential, that of possessing the ability to beat a man, normally the full-back and more often than not his mate the defensive midfielder/winger. Brennan and Sheedy, though very fine players, would rather hit a diagonal than take the defender on. It is just a case of different styles and mine didn't fit in with the manager.

This type of football didn't suit me either. All I wanted to do was get the ball and run at people. I wanted to beat two or three players and cross the ball for the centre-forward. I wanted to excite. I did not want to be involved in football that defended first and did not have the bottle to take the game to the opposition. Whether Sharpe detected this through a cognitive process or whether he arrived at it by instinct does not matter. He came to the right conclusion regarding his involvement of me and so things had to change. It is worth me recording, in fairness to Mark Brennan, that he openly admitted that he couldn't play in the orthodox left-wing slot and was more suited to 20 yards further down at left-back. He was called upon to play behind me in this position in the odd emergency and it worked very well. He had that rare ability, missing in 90 per cent of full-backs, of being able to pass the ball five yards or 55 yards, a very rare luxury in any side. Instead, both Joe and then Sharpy persisted with Neil Pointon, a player of proven ability but who had adopted the Everton method of crashing the big diagonal ball and ignoring the winger standing five yards away from him, but, as they say, that's another story. Mark Brennan never said much in the changing room and was very much a dark horse, keeping himself to himself, and we don't know where he is now.

Results got worse and crowds dwindled as season 1994–95 petered out and we narrowly avoided relegation. The jury was still out on Graeme Sharpe – it was his first season and he hadn't been appointed until November, so this, quite rightly, allowed him the benefit of the doubt. There wasn't any magic in his pre-season, however, and ultimately no getting away from hard work. His tour of Scotland was a good excuse to return to his home town but I didn't go, opting out through injury to my right knee. It's a pity because I really like Scotland. I had wondered why, over the length of my career, my knee had swollen periodically. It was particularly bad on hard ground. I was to find out several months later, at the end of my time, that it was an old posterior cruciate injury, probably traceable to a solo run 10 years before which had gone horribly wrong. I wouldn't have featured on the trip anyway, even though I'd tried to put everything into the new season and trained with a smile on my face. I knew I was coming to the end. As the new season 1995–96 stumbled on, results got steadily worse, but it didn't seem to matter and I was frozen out all the more. I was again to be found playing in the reserves, hoping some clubs would come in for me, but even if they did I knew that I wouldn't be informed. I soldiered on, captaining the team that had won promotion to the Pontin's First Division, courtesy of the most outrageous fluke, when I went to cross a ball in the last game of the season against Burnley at Turf Moor to win 1–0 in the 85th minute. It had little impact on the management. My commitment hadn't meant much because the gaffer wasn't there to witness it. Oldham were still getting beaten with outstanding consistency, and the club was looking at oblivion like never before. I played one final game at Stalybridge and thought, 'That's it, you bunch of losers, I'm off.'

The following morning I approached Sharpe and Stott with my plan. I asked the pair if they would consider paying up my contract and allowing me to retire. There was also a verbal agreement that the club would take my weekly salary and use it to pay the most-promising homegrown youngsters and not splash out on a quick-fix buy, thus wasting the money. How did they spend the £1,800 per week? They spent £180,000 on a midfielder called Toddy Orlygsson. Still, they duly accepted my plan and signed my release papers, although Stott did resemble a guppy fish while Sharpe looked sheepish. Had a player ever approached a club's hierarchy before with this sort of request? Probably, but it was unusual.

I had not been totally honest — anyone with half a brain could see that there was no way that I was going to retire, and all I was doing was trying to resurrect my career, which had been brought to a halt. People forget this about me. They think of Oldham and Rick Holden and only remember the crosses and the goals and the laughs. They don't remember this ugly bit at the end. I had a couple of irons in the fire but nothing concrete. I didn't think for one minute that they would believe my story that I wanted to retire to concentrate on a new physiotherapy career. It was an easy way of creating a quick buck — a £20,000 signing on fee from Blackpool and £30,000 from Oldham within a week, which meant £50,000 at the flick of a switch. That's what I call good business, and finally I did something for myself after months of misery. I felt that I deserved it, after all the things that I had helped the club achieve and all the shit that I had had to put up with, and without complaining either. It can't have been a shock to the Oldham management when two weeks later I emerged in tangerine by the seaside, but it was a bit of a shock when they bought the Icelander almost immediately. Still, what did I care now? As far as I was concerned, I was going to enjoy a few twilight years before hanging up my boots. I'd always had faith in my ability to start again, and I saw potential in Blackpool football club.

Relegation beckoned for the Latics and duly occurred, and I felt a real sense of loss. As I left the ground, I took a sideways glance as I headed down the A627M and thought it ironic that I'd had so much to do with their rise and fall but that there was little I could do about it now.

At Blackpool we were flying under Sam Allardyce's guidance and I was just happy to be playing again. Such a long time out of first-team football meant my match fitness was a little way short, but nonetheless I was enjoying myself once again. Blackpool, now more famous for its dirty beaches and tourism tat than a once-legendary team, is still buzzing at night time and held its attraction for me. This, after all, was the town where I'd woken up several years earlier stark naked on a showroom bed without a clue before or since about how I'd got there, and no one seemed to be taking any interest, as though it was an everyday experience. I loved the people of Blackpool's indifference to outrageous behaviour. They have to be like that, I suppose, as they champion the place as a party town. It was no different now. I'd had plenty of good times in Blackpool as a young lad from as early as 15 years old. It was the place we visited for a day by the sea, even from Yorkshire. Skipton is nearer to the Lancastrian coast than places like Filey, Scarborough and Whitby. These Yorkshire resorts are some 40 miles further away along a road which hadn't been widened since Dick Turpin's day. They are about as lively now as they were in the famous highwayman's day and are now visited only by teams of mods and rockers on their various machines.

On one famous occasion we visited Blackpool under the guise of Saltaire cricket club for a pre-season friendly. Following the uneventful game, there was a huge piss-up around the town and, naturally enough, we got split up into various groups on our tour of the pubs. My team was the last to arrive at the bus rendezvous by some minutes, the reason being that the billboard we'd nicked was 12ft by 4ft and weighed a ton. Everyone helped to prise it onto the bus: after all, it did say, 'Today's visitors to Stanley Park – SALTAIRE from the Bradford League!' As I dragged it along the road back into Embsay like some kind of trophy, I was stopped and quizzed by the local constable, but when he realised that it was me and thought about the amount of paperwork involved he just left me to it with a shake of the head. Incidentally, the board is still at my dad's and is used as a tool board on his garage wall. Yes, Blackpool holds quite a few famous stories involving certain footballers.

At the same time as returning full-time pro football I was trying to combine it with physiotherapy at the Yorkshire clinic, which included some physio for the rugby league team Bradford Northern, later to be named the Bradford Bulls. It would have worked in an ideal world, but this arrangement proved impossible even though Big Sam was really supportive at first. We were about to have our second child and my wife Jean was suffering. She was becoming very tired and the placental problem she had with Will was beginning to occur again with Alex. I also became run down and tired, and it was very obvious that we couldn't continue as we were. I had been superhuman 10 years earlier, combining a Leeds Carnegie degree in debauchery with playing for Halifax Town, but now I was in the real world of kids, mortgages and no sleep and ultimately I began to crack. The Yorkshire clinic hadn't exactly been straight with me either. What had been agreed as a few hours in order to develop a new physiotherapy service for professional sportsmen in the local area, using my name to give it some credibility, was, in the end, a fallacy. I ended up doing dogsbody rotational undergraduate work plus evening work for the Bradford reserve team. I found myself running on for a bunch of rugby league hopefuls in more godforsaken northern depositaries. This wasn't me – I was a player. Performing physiotherapy for psychotic thugs in my spare time was for those who couldn't play anymore because they were knackered from all the days playing. The car journeys were endless as well, and I found myself constantly battling against the clock due to the ridiculous infrastructure that is our national road network.

I was the blade runner, ready for burn out, and something had to give. After a two-day bout of the flu, I jacked it in at the clinic, much to their surprise. And I really enjoyed telling them, too. The people there had abused my services and now I was off, unrepentant that I wasn't giving them a month's notice. Let you who are unlucky enough to happen to stumble upon this literary masterpiece take just one lesson from me. Work hard in life, but beware of the bastards who take you for granted and put upon you. Before you know, they'll be riding rough-shod over you. Don't let this happen. Don't let the bastards grind you down. I announced to Sam that I wanted to sign for another year and totally commit myself to footy, which pleased both him and my wife, and we could look forward to a good Christmas and a bright New Year.

Then came the cruel twist of fate. Two injuries, one after the other, effectively ended my career prematurely. The first, the most painful dead leg I'd ever sustained, which landed me in a full-length bandage from thigh to ankle known as a Robert Jones, occurred against Bradford City at home. I just couldn't get away from that blasted city. The resultant bleed into the muscle set me back for six weeks, causing me to miss the Christmas fixtures and costing me some appearance money. I made my comeback in the reserves at, surprisingly enough, Bradford City. I did very well, only playing the first half and then being pulled out in preparation for the first team on the Saturday. We settled down into a rhythm and headed for promotion.

I had teamed up with an old pal from the Oldham glory days, Andy Barlow. Andy played behind me at left-back, and we were taking the piss out of the teams at this level. I enjoyed delivering my approach to football for Blackpool, and it seemed to be having a positive effect. I single-handedly wound up the whole of the Crewe first team and fans in our 2–1 win at Gresty Road. Then I was escorted from the field by the police at Wycombe for much the same thing in another away win and in a classic straight out of *Monty Python*. I incurred the wrath of the Brighton faithful during our win at the Hove. We were reduced to 10 men when my Oldham mate was asked to leave the arena for two X-rated challenges, which he was occasionally prone to pull off. I remember one such challenge in particular down at Ipswich in 1990, in a crucial tie which saw us reach the First Division, when out of the blue he sent Romeo Zondervan over the dug-out and onto the approaching manager John Lyle. He didn't return to action. Because of Andy's misdemeanor I ended up playing left-back, which is a groovy position in that you have loads of the ball, and in the final few minutes I was once again in possession. We had won a throw-in in the depths of Brighton's half and, as I held it in my hands, none of my teammates volunteered their services to receive the ball. The ref politely told me to get on with it and I could see Liam Brady and his bench gesticulating wildly at my time-wasting. There was only one thing I could do: I flung it into the crowd over the small angle of the corner of the pitch between the touch line and the goal line for a goal-kick. The reaction, which I can only describe as bordering on epileptic, took everyone by surprise, including the ref, who ran over to me blowing his whistle and gesticulating until he came to his senses and awarded a goal-kick. To compound matters, the ball ended up with the Blackpool supporters who, true to form, refused to hand it back over to the goalkeeper. By this time Mr Brady, Brighton's gaffer, was at his wits' end and heading for the ref's diary, whereas my teammates were just left open-mouthed. This unique brand of rule-bending was helping, but then the twist of fate occurred that was, if I'd have been paranoid, beginning to become special to me.

In the return game at home to Brighton — it must be teams which begin with the letter 'B' which are the jinx — came the curtain on my adventure in football. In an exciting game most memorable for a long-range spectacular from Mickey Mellon, I was ignominiously stretchered off following a challenge on the right-hand edge of the penalty area. I remember making a run down the right-hand side of the box and setting myself ready to cross it into the side netting when suddenly I felt tremendous pain followed by a loud crack which my chauffeur, Meadows, heard from the directors' box. After a couple of thousand giga seconds it dawned on me that something pretty serious might have happened to my knee, but it failed to register with anyone else. A corner was awarded and players, officials, fans and the management waited for me to get up and take it. Looking back, I can't blame them, because things were coming home to roost and maybe people thought I was crying wolf. Even in my death throes I'd managed to get in a dive, for which I had become infamous, and my cynicism returned to haunt me. I was never a diver like you get today, but if I was hit and couldn't score I would go down.

This isn't how it was supposed to end. I should have been walking off to a standing ovation at Oldham under the guidance of Andy Ritchie, not lying in an empty treatment room under a rickety 1930s stand in north-west England, which, like my knee, looked like it might have collapsed around me like my career. Blackpool was, like me, a relic, and like me it had had its day. Suddenly I was contemplating the end. It was the longest half-hour of my year, rather like when you're in the boozer waiting for a mate who is late and you don't know anyone.

I was eventually patched up and sent home on crutches. I was invited to a public house in St Anne's to meet some Blackpool and Brighton fans, so, undaunted and in considerable pain, I went to the show. It was easy really, I was nearly always with my driver, either Bill Illingworth (Mick Hillary) or Meadows (Keith 'Woody' Woodhead). Although the alcohol seemed to be working as a painkiller, I couldn't stop thinking about the incident and my future. Normally when you take a knock the consequences wear off as the alcohol goes down, but this one didn't. This had always been the way. I belonged to and emerged from the era where no matter what level you played, it was always out for a few beers afterwards with the lads. It is different now. After a match it's a high-carbohydrate-replacement drink followed by some food and a couple of pints of water and then back home to bed on your own. This is lifestyle à l'Italia and was adopted by Big Sam at the seaside. Following the game we had to endure his summary of the performance while trying to choke back a thick, sickly milkshake. Then you had to make sure that you'd had a dinner before heading for home. What if you were going out for a meal later, I once enquired? No answer was forthcoming. This puts me in mind of the reaction of the Italians when Graeme Souness arrived on the scene in Torino. Apocryphally, following the first game for the once Turin giants, Souness allegedly went into the bar and to the jaw-clanging amazement of his colleagues, not to mention his gaffer, sorted out his thirst by 'yanning' back half a gallon of alcohol like he'd just lost four games of coin spoof for his local rugby club. Paul Gascoigne purportedly courted similar reaction at Lazio with his post-match entertainment. It was suggested to him that perhaps he should drink wine instead of lager, but when they saw him down the wine like a kid gulping orange cordial on a hot summer's day, they quickly recommended he stick to the lager.

The following morning it occurred to me that the injury was indeed very serious. The big give-away I have found in my professional experience is gross swelling, pain and the inability to move. It obviously needed a scan and arthroscope to get to the bottom of it. This was Blackpool, however, not Blackburn. The club was in disarray as the chairman was doing time. The gauleiter was pulling the purse strings tighter and the management were therefore operating with their hands tied behind their backs. I was left in the caring hands of the physio, Mark Taylor, who was as clueless as me at the time as we'd both just qualified at the same time at Salford and knew nothing. We suspected anterior cruciate ligament damage, but had no way of confirming it. It is different now. With experience you can tell a cruciate by the way a person walks. With cycling it began to settle down and I was rehabilitated to a stage where we thought we could test it out in the reserves at Bolton. There was a panic on as we hadn't won a game since my injury and Oxford were catching up with an unbelievable run, but it should never have been tested this early. After five minutes I twisted and turned for a ball, and down I went like one of Fred Dibner's chimneys. It was hopeless. We finally persuaded the club that it might be prudent to have a scan on the left knee, and while we were at it we might as well get the right knee done at the same time as I was still having the odd inflammatory reaction from this on hard ground. The results were both amazing and conclusive. It revealed a complete rupture of the anterior cruciate in the left knee and also a complete rupture of my posterior cruciate in my right knee. It said that it was about 10 years old, and I couldn't recall any incident way back then.

The posterior cruciate is a complimentary and stronger ligament and gets its name from its position, cruciate meaning cross. It helps to stabilise the knee joint in forwards, backward and rotational movements, and once this complex is damaged in any way the knee can become grossly unstable. I couldn't recall any incident but then finally came up with the Exeter City game in 1986 when I was playing for Halifax. I had ended up on my arse, bringing my heel down on top of the ball with enough violence to rupture the ligament. I'd carried on regardless, as you did in those days in case someone took your place and did you out of a few weeks' appearance money. I could recall the following day at my bedsit, marooned not just by a sea of empty beer cans and road signs, but because I was unable to move my right leg more than about an inch. I got Melt to ring the club and the manager dispatched a posse to round me up for treatment. It took them about two hours to find me in Headingley and about one hour to extract me from the morass of crap in my room. It seems so long ago now that it feels like it happened to a different person.

I was confronted by the hard facts of football life. A once-dynamic winger now reduced to a wading bird. The options were harsh, too. What had I done? Firstly,

I'd walked away from Manchester City when pushed, then I'd walked out on Oldham when ostracised. Now I was on a sticky wicket with Blackpool with only a few months contract left, knowing that any rehabilitation for cruciate would be at least six to eight months. It was very unlikely that they would stick by me in any financial manner. As it was, they only paid what amounted to petrol money in my real contract anyway. I suppose I could have bummed my way around some GM Vauxhall or Uni-Bond club in the hope that I might pick up a contract there and then return to the professional game when or if fit. Things were so uncertain. I had to move quickly, though, to declare my injury to the Football League for compensation and pension matters. What was I to do? Then, out of the blue, the Isle of Man appeared like a boat from behind Manannan mac Lir's cloak of mist.

A woman with whom I'd had a run in or disagreement surprisingly approached me with an advert for physiotherapy on the Isle of Man at Noble's hospital as she knew that I was keen on the place. This particular lady had encouraged me to take the post at the Yorkshire clinic, and now this. It led her into being the most active careers advisor I'd ever had. Even following a personality clash we'd had several weeks earlier she had produced this advert for Manx land. It was obvious really. She had got me the job at the Yorkshire clinic, but decided that I wasn't quite the material she wanted, so perhaps it was best if she exiled me to a foreign post, rather like the practices of ancient Rome when they used to send naughty centurions to the outer reaches of the empire – past Hadrian's Wall. She followed this up with a phone call to the physiotherapy department at Noble's warning them about me. The garbled message I received several months later alluded to me being difficult and highly opinionated. This character flaw, which I call honesty, has got me into many scrapes in the past and no doubt will do so again in the future. When asked my opinion there are, of course, two answers – the right one and the wrong one. The right one is, however, is not generally the one people want to hear. What's more, interestingly, blunt opinion is seen as arrogance and any criticism on an objective level is taken as personal. In the end you just shut up and curse under your breath. It is the same in football. Any individual expression of thought, no matter how mild, is perceived as being dangerous and radical.

I arrived at Noble's hospital basically to start from scratch as a physio. I had picked the best place in the world to do this for someone of my age. I was not about to get heaps of pressure piled upon me by some 1950s-trained dragon who was more interested in dress code and subservience than the ability to do the job. I would be able to ease into the task, which is what I did eventually, learning the profession from top to bottom at more or less my own pace. Physiotherapy, like most professions, is only really mastered through hands-on practical experience. You can read about it, pontificate about it and observe it, but you'll not understand it until you've worked out in the field for a few years. This is what I had decided to do before re-emerging into the field of professional football in the future (I thought), that is if anyone would have me. I made a conscious decision to make sure I had covered everything I could, and therefore know how to fix any problems that I might be faced with in the future.

Knowing that I was helpless to alleviate Blackpool's immediate plight I retired to Majorca with the family to sadly watch them throw it all away, finally getting rolled by Bradford City in the Play-offs. Blackpool should have got promotion that year and would have been far better placed to get into the Premier League earlier than now, but the board sacked Big Sam Allardyce, possibly the best manager they'd had for many a long year, and then they stagnated until 2009. With this came the end of any re-entry into the game from an Isle of Man base. It would have been possible to commute to the Pleasure Beach from Manx land, but not to Notts County where Sam got himself a new and deserved job. My experience of English travel had hardened me against any such thoughts, and in any case I'd always had a nightmare at the County ground so I didn't fancy it. It's not so bad having a nightmare at a particular away ground in a one-off situation, or even having the odd bogey ground or two; however, it is another when your own patch is your bogey ground. Playing badly every other week at home is not, as we say in the game, 'the one'. Another thing to consider was whether I wanted to play for a team in the lower division not fully fit and as a target for younger, faster, better-looking players to kick me up hill and down dale. The answer was no.

Rest was the order of the day, and after my recent experiences at Blackpool I had a bad taste in my mouth. Blackpool was back-to-basics football, which is not what I had had in mind at the age of 31. Little more than petrol money as a wage, endless coach journeys on the day of a game because the directors wouldn't pay for overnight stops and endless moronic practice on throw-ins and kick-off routines was hard work to say the least. The club could not match Sam's commitment, or mine for that matter, and in the end I guess we were both better off out of it. What had happened to a once great club? What had happened to all these once great football clubs of the North West, many of which were founder members of the Football League? I can tell you that the real underlying problem has been a failure to move with times. Why am I so confident in my assessment? Because I've seen it at first hand. As I have mentioned, any new ideas in these clubs were seen as dangerous and revolutionary and going against the grain as to how things had always been done. To be fair, these clubs are making a bit of a fight-back and it is good to see, but can they win anything and break the big club dominance? I would love to see it, but I doubt it.

I'd gone up and down the mountain in a whistle-stop 10 years and had come back to the point where I'd set off. It had been illuminating but not, I have to say, a journey we couldn't have predicted. I was a boy from the Dales who played rugby and was thought capable of making anything in life, let alone in sport, according to my headmaster. But there I was. I had shown the world how to cross a ball and had reached the top of the domestic game. Time to try life outside the stadium.

# eight

## Sunset City

The aircraft constantly buzzing down the runway and escaping out of Blackpool into the skies above the Irish Sea was more than I could stand. I had suggested to Jean that we should go and live in the Isle of Man to make a fresh start back in September 1995, a suggestion that was met with raised eyebrows resembling Wallace's canine friend. Having subsequently joined Blackpool I was tantalisingly close, made worse by the fact that the airport is directly adjacent to the training ground. My plan of working part-time at the Yorkshire clinic on the outskirts of Bradford and playing a full part in Blackpool's promotion push had collapsed around my ears. It was just too much to try to combine the two. I could cope with dual stuff 10 years earlier but not now. There must be a better way of doing things and a better lifestyle altogether and I mulled these things over as another plane droned over my head out towards the west.

It was by now mid-March 1996 and my knee had finally been diagnosed with the aid of an MRI scan as a ruptured anterior cruciate ligament, which meant that I would not play again in the current campaign. The scan should have taken place immediately and we could have prevented further damage if we had discovered the extent of the injury straight away, but, as I mentioned, Mark and I were newly qualified at the time so we made mistakes. Something had to be done about it now, but such were the financial restrictions at Blackpool (I think that I had more money than they did in their current account) that this scan was done under duress. I kept receiving the bill months later asking me to pay for the scan and the consultancy work of the radiographer, which would be fairly unique and unprecedented in the modern game.

Would I stay on at Blackpool without a contract (my present one would run out in July) and try to rehabilitate myself, or would I take the offer of a job in the Isle of Man and call it quits on the game? We decided to go to Majorca for a week, or rather my wife decided it for us, which, with a new three-month-old baby, was a bit of a nightmare. It gave me time to mull things over. The chances of full recovery from cruciate damage are becoming increasingly better nowadays; however, it is still a risky business. If only I knew then what I do now about cruciate rehab then I might well have made a different decision. The Isle of Man seemed to offer more security in the long term, and I don't think I believed that I would be out for long. If Big Sam was still there the following season I thought I might have been able to alter my tack. Against this was the fact that Blackpool's record of looking after its players wasn't exactly a case study in the acts of kindness brochure for human rights, and given that the chairman had been sent down, things did not look good. The long-term upshot of all this was disastrous for Blackpool. I could see it all coming and because I was incapacitated I decided to go to Manx land for the intermediate period and observe the soap opera from a distance. An event which swung it for me occurred when I got back from Majorca.

Blackpool were, as I have mentioned, on the verge of promotion and needed a win to secure automatic promotion. I decided to go down and give support at as many away games as I could, and the next and very decisive one was at Chesterfield. It is one of the most godforsaken 'off the beaten track' grounds to get to in the Football League and the ground hadn't been updated since it was built. The car park is small and so ridiculously ineffective that it rivals Naples airport for the worst design in the history of car parks. Unfortunately I hadn't been to Chesterfield for so long that I had forgotten this fact, so it was with some naivety that I asked Blackpool to organise a car park pass for the evening's game. It was normal procedure to get the host club to accommodate visiting dignitaries, but often the game's hierarchy does not include players in this important bracket. Blackpool informed me that there weren't any tickets for cars for players or directors at Chesterfield. At Oldham I was treated like royalty by our secretary, Terry Cale, who would give me a director's pass whenever I wanted one. The Oldham directors, being classical drinkers, used to go to away games on the team bus so that they could get pissed up before and after the game in the directors' bar.

Blackpool was being run by a female secretary who was harder-faced than any bloke that I had ever come up against in the game. When I first went to sign on six months earlier she had a copy of the *Playfair* football book in front of her. She tried to pull my achievements apart, suggesting that I was over the hill and should be grateful for having been offered the poxy contract that she tried to fob off on me. Needless to say I walked out. It was no surprise then when I saw the chain of events unfold in front of me that evening. Meadows, my driver, finally found a place to park up in the back streets of Chesterfield about a mile from the ground after a failed attempt to wangle our way into the car park was blocked by a jobsworth official. It says something about the importance of players in the game. We are just scum gladiators who are constantly replaceable, and the directors are the really important people in the game and so have all the privileges. We strolled up to the ground, via a local boozer, just in time to witness a posse of cars being ushered into the ground like a state visit to Downing Street. Who should get out but the secretary and all her entourage. I won't mention her name, not because I am scared of legal action, but because she doesn't deserve to get a mention in a football book. That would be an insult to every football player who has ever sweated their guts out on the professional scene. She swept by me, giving me the complete swerve, and didn't show an ounce of emotion. She knew that I had rumbled her, though. Unfortunately we lost the match, but at least she is out of the game now and how I hope she falls. By all accounts she did, but sadly so did Blackpool. Losing the game meant losing the automatic spot for promotion.

Following the Majorca trip, which was a John Candy *Planes, Trains and Automobiles* spectacular in which every conceivable irritation occurred, I decided to pack up my things and leave. Once again it was time to go. I began boxing up my worldly possessions, which took about four weeks of more or less constant sorting. I had collected so much stuff, some of it valuable, some sentimental, but most of it crap, that I was expecting a visit from the kleptomaniacs' society and the presentation of a special award.

I had several bites from people interested in my house but nothing substantial, so we decided to rent it out to a nice family and simultaneously rented a place in Douglas. It was one of those barely soundproof cardboard boxes, but it would have to do. On 10 May 1996 I transported the basic possessions in a transit van across the Irish Sea on the *King Orry* ship. It was the weekend of the worst FA Cup Final of all time between Liverpool and Manchester United. Neither side seemed to want to win the game and neither seemed capable, and it was left to Eric the Seagull to volley in the winner. Liverpool made the mistake of turning up in hideous white suits, and it cost them. They played like prats, but worse, they looked like prats. Finally, on 22 May I left my beloved Yorkshire and headed for a new world full of anticipation.

The word for gossip in the Isle of Man is 'skeet', and this is a national pastime. Thus, it didn't take long for the word to get around that an ex-professional footballer was working at the local hospital. Very soon offers were coming in from the clubs on the island inviting me to play for them, assuming for some strange reason that the first thing I would want to do when arriving on the rock was to resume playing. You would have thought that the first thing on my mind was football, but then the populace thinks that's all a soccer player thinks about. A couple of plods from the local constabulary came around to the out-patients' department to apply some heat. The words were along the line of, 'Come and play for us and meet the right kind of people.' Did this also mean that I would be arrested or exempt if I was caught in an uncompromising situation while at large on the island? My stock answer to all the inquiries was that I hadn't had chance to think about it and would therefore need to look around the place before making any decisions. The same stood for housing and in which town we were going to set up our home base. Advice was freely offered without needing to ask. All and sundry got involved and usually began with 'Where are you staying?' When I replied that I was renting in Farmhill the response was, 'Oh yes, nice place, convenient for Douglas isn't it?' I thought everywhere on the island was fairly convenient for Douglas. I didn't think much of Farmhill beyond functional, as the estate could have been anywhere.

During the summer, my wife and I trailed around the rock looking for the best spot to create our new headquarters. This was another peculiar thing, together with the footy, which helped shape my decision. Nine out of 10 people who had asked me about domicile and footy choice had said to keep well clear of Peel. That's odd, I thought. I'd spent most of the summer down there on its class little beach with the kids and I reckoned that the town, or 'city' as it can be called, had everything going for it and was ideal for us. It has a beautiful old castle steeped in history, a fine cathedral, and both a primary and a large secondary school with plenty of playing fields. It has plenty of pubs, a good golf club and a football club that looked like it meant business, and the only faults that I could find were the lack of a swimming pool and curry house (it has these essentials now). The town itself reminded me of parts of Cornwall with its narrow organic streets, which have developed naturally out from the harbour to prevent the wind howling up them and to provide cover and confusion for the smugglers. Yes, this was a superb little place and the natives seemed friendly enough on the surface. We had spent two months on the place and still not found the Utopian place to live or the most suitable building to fit all our rubbish in. Don't get me wrong, there are plenty of nice villages and towns on the island, but none with all my requirements, except perhaps Ramsey, which could have a lot going for it in my opinion.

Since 1984 I had had 11 different houses. Each had something but none of them had everything. I wanted plenty of rooms, a couple of bathrooms, cellars, a double garage, gardens front and back, a sea view and it had to be within walking distance of the pub. We looked at a superb house in a hamlet called Maughold and were very tempted by it until I discovered that Maughold was boozerless, the nearest watering hole being in Ramsey several miles away. 'I don't think we'll buy this Jean – dry rot – needs too much doing.' People kept on offering us their wisdom of not living in Peel and it teaches you something about psychology. When people consistently run a place down and yet offer up no real explanation for it, it means the opposite. There must be some reason for running a place or a person down, but it all begins to get a little tiresome and in the end tells you more about the idiot doing the 'knocking' than the place or person concerned. One must remember that the majority of people are not mental giants, most are frightened and most harbour irrational prejudices born out of jealousy. Hence, when a collection of half-wits tell me not to do something, I usually do it as they have acted as my quality control. The real reason for people trying to steer me clear of Peel is deep-rooted and two-fold. Most people on the island are now not indigenous Manx, the percentage is now around 60 per cent 'foreigners' and 40 per cent Manx born. Very few of those who have come over have settled in Peel; they think that it is too Manx and not busy enough, and they prefer the hustle and bustle of Douglas. They have an unhealthy distrust of the Manxman and prefer to stay in Douglas. The native Manxman, on the other hand, either fears the Peel Manx or is jealous of him. I could not believe the crap I have heard over something and nothing on the island regarding this particular topic. That's a small island for you, but it is safe to say that if you can fit in at Peel you'll fit in anywhere, and I decided that I'd have a go at that. I like a challenge.

There is a beauty about Peel that is difficult to see now in many parts of mainland Britain. Kids can play out without fear. I often see them playing unsupervised – football, bike riding, fishing or on the beach. The horror stories in England mean that you would never take your eyes off your kids for a second if you could avoid it.

One morning when I arrived at work there were two letters waiting for me. One was an invite to join Peel football club from a man called Paul Barlow, while the other was from the dragon from Blackpool. This was accompanied by a bill from a hotel and country club in the Midlands citing roughly £2,000 worth of criminal damage. I stood accused of causing fire damage to a rug, some ornamental reeds, a leather chair and the theft of a wooden pig. I promptly wrote back denying all knowledge of the incident. What had happened was that earlier in the year Blackpool was presented with free weekend on the fixture calendar, not out of kindness from the League, but because we'd perished in the FA Cup. The gaffer, Big Sam Allardyce, decided to take us on a morale-boosting trip to the Black Country for a friendly against the Throstles of West Brom and a jolly old knees-up. The trouble was that after beating Alan 'youth' Buckley's team things got a bit out of hand. We began with a few gentle cocktails at 6pm, then strolled to the local through the snow. Upon returning, it was snowing quite heavily and by the time we reached the hotel we were somewhat on the frozen side and requiring some heat internally and externally. The internal situation was quickly rectified with a large one, whereas we had a problem with the outside as the fire was almost out. Beer mats were not in plentiful enough supply to ignite the huge log that was left half-charred, so we had to improvise on the kindling front. There was only one thing for it, and the ornamental reeds in the large urn in the corner of the room looked like ideal firelighters. I carefully folded them down into the fire grate and whuuuffffft! They went up in moments. The heat and light given off was so tremendous that it lit up the whole room and then on went the logs, which caught easily. I had majored in pyromania at Leeds so this was child's play. It also freed up the urn as a toilet for the rest of the night, but they never mentioned that on the itemised bill. 'Wooden pig £120, carpet £1,800, ornamental reeds £450, urn full of piss £350.' Not a mention of it. I had noticed a small burn on the edge of the rug but there was no extensive damage, especially amounting to a claim of these proportions. The hotel was obviously trying to pull a fast one.

A couple of weeks later I received a letter threatening legal action, so I called in my solicitor, instructing him to inform the relative authorities that if I had hypothetically turned into an alcoholic pyromaniac, I certainly hadn't caused that amount of damage and certainly was not a pig thief, wooden or otherwise. I never heard from them again, so my solicitor must have done the trick. I think perhaps that the Blackpool secretary met her match with my solicitor, Mr Mewis. As for the wooden pig, I know where that went and the little boy who owns it has a father who looks a bit like a rutting wild boar when he turns out for his team. Petty theft is rife among pro footballers and has something to do with having your eye on the main chance. I can vividly recall one of Joe Royle's addresses prior to us setting off to a game one Saturday lunch time: 'I've just had the manager of the hotel onto me. Apparently someone has pinched one of the plastic ducks out of one of the hotel bedrooms, so I want the thing recovering and bringing down to the front.' There was silence followed by some smothered smirks, but the threat must have been strong enough as about half a dozen ducks were handed over. Being one step ahead I had snaffled two, and although I handed one in the other is still sitting there, pride of place, on my bath side.

Finally we found the ideal home in Peel with all our requirements although I probably went over the top on the pub access front. I can walk to eight boozers and six clubs within five minutes. I had an inkling that it would be Peel AFC. It is the biggest club on the island and it has a classic history in that, like many professional counterparts in England, it was founded in the 1880s at a hotel, in this case the Royal Hotel in Peel. The club has won more trophies than any other club in Manx football history and enjoys the largest and most fanatical following. This was the ideal place then to settle down, take stock and start again.

Due to my recent injury I'd not expected to be able to play any football and was just hoping to be able to contribute in some way to Peel and Isle of Man football in general. I was offered constructive surgery by Mr Steve Bollen, orthopaedic surgeon extraordinaire from Bradford, but instead opted to rehabilitate it myself following rest. I do repair quite well, and the knowledge that I'd played for 10 years with a ruptured posterior cruciate ligament in my right knee without being aware of it had encouraged me.

It was with some apprehension that I began training with Peel and decided to give it a go in the pre-season friendlies. I played in all six games, failed to score but made a few, and then embarked on an unprecedented run of 50 games, a record number of games for a club in one season for Manx football. This was as long as some professional seasons, but I managed it and, incredibly, at a goal a game ratio. We had terrific support from the locals of Peel, even taking a remarkable 1,300 fans to the FA Cup Final, in which we finally triumphed in the second replay. My cruciate had stood up with only the occasional cartilage pain, and even that's gone now. It began to play tricks with my mind, however – had I left the game too early? What the hell was I doing working in a hospital when I should be playing football? Circumstances had gone against me but I suppose it was my fault, and I had to be thankful for small mercies, for what I had already been lucky enough to have experienced and achieved already. I was grateful that I could still play football and for a club and community that cared passionately about its team. As thankful for all those experiences in the pro-game as I am, and for the financial reward I had received as well, it still didn't seem to help. What used to bring it home, and even worse with the advent of Sky television showing every game in England's four divisions over the course of the weekend, was seeing my mates still playing. It did, I must admit, get me down a little. The real things you miss are the outdoor life and feeling of fitness and health through training every day, the banter and camaraderie with the lads day-in day-out in the dressing room, and the buzz of playing in front of big crowds. At least Peel had a large following and I wasn't reduced to playing Parks Department football in front of one man and his hound. What had I now, though? Working indoors in a hospital, surrounded by sick and unhealthy people, and no banter from colleagues.

It appeared to me that a pre-requisite for working in the health service in physiotherapy, radiography and occupational therapy was to be as fat and overweight as possible and to have the personality of a wardrobe. You couldn't discuss the previous evening's footy match or the continued disruptive state of English cricket with anyone apart from the odd person or the gloating Aussie locum. Maybe I'm being a bit harsh again. The workers at the local hospital, and most hospitals for that matter, are very dedicated on the whole. It's just that they were more 'whole' than most. The receptionists in physio were nice though, well they were to me, and more caring than some of the staff and a damn site more fun. The hospital did well for me. It honed my skills and got me up to speed, and ultimately I did well for them. The troubles with the NHS on the Isle of Man are the same as in the rest of the country in that it is under-staffed (apart from the management – more chiefs than indians), under-paid when compared to other services and under-valued by local and central government. The trouble with being a physiotherapist is that it is as poorly paid as nursing (indeed, it is less so now) with less recognition. All we ever hear is how under-paid nurses are and how over-worked doctors are, yet no mention is made of physiotherapy. Working with the

NHS you have the opportunity of meeting the generally demanding and often obnoxious and ungrateful public and there can only be one winner. You have very little time to see and deal with an ever-increasing waiting list of outpatients and it requires a fair number of full-time physios all seeing about four patients per hour. At Noble's I was left with two full-time personnel and two part-timers to deal with an outpatient demand of 75,000 people. I had no option but to throw myself whole-heartedly into the job, and we managed to get the waiting list down from 10 weeks to 10 days, but at a hell of a price. Eventually, enough was enough and I got burnt out. I didn't enjoy going to work anymore. I was tired, had developed backache for the first time in my life and, to be honest, when I looked at my wage packet I thought long and hard. Did I want to listen to some pillock whingeing on about buttock pain when I felt like this, while the management held endless meetings about meaningless crap? Management, whether at a football club or in the NHS, take the workers for granted, even in today's over-sensitive world. If you do a good job there aren't any thanks, and if you break down they drop you like a broken toy. They are two very similar professions who treat you the same.

I had come to the end of the road working for an untouchable system or possibly for anyone else. That was it. The scales were beginning to fall from my eyes. I had to work either for myself or, if not totally on my terms, no longer for a faceless system. This had all coincided with the expected arrival of our third velociraptor in May 1999 and the other two raptors, William and Alex, were fast becoming a handful. Then there was the golf, which currently was costing me £27 per round – I'd had 10 rounds last year and this had to change. Thus, after a little thought, in which I nearly turned my back on physio completely, I accepted an invitation to work in the private sector, starting at 8am and on the first tee at 3pm. Not bad. This would give me more time and energy to work on the football, which as anyone, professional or amateur, will tell you, is a never-ending job as manager.

The previous season (1998–99) had been a disaster at Peel. We had won the Manx Charity Shield, the traditional season curtain-raiser in most Leagues it seems, and from there it went downhill. It resulted in the management duo being rather cruelly dismissed, which led to some civil unrest with emotions running very high.

Mind you, one win from 10 League games out of a total of just 24 was cause for concern. Some stupid things were said by all parties, and I must admit I was very surprised to discover the depth that feelings ran to in such a small community as Peel. Then again, I have come to realise that in Peel, football is a very serious proposition indeed. Where else would you get a population of 3,500 people taking 1,300 to a Final? It is on the same scale as Burnley, who used to get crowds (and still could) of 30,000 in a town of 70,000. Imagine this scaled up in a city like Liverpool or Leeds – fanatical is the word which readily springs to mind. I became caretaker manager for the remainder of the season, and with help from many, but particularly a young lad, Kelvin Dawson, who, at 23 years old, had been carrying the can of running the side with tremendous maturity and strength since the uproar, we pulled clear of the danger zone.

From 1996 until 2003 I was heavily involved with Peel as manager, assistant, physio, coach and player. It proved very successful and naturally very enjoyable, and I shall tell you a story from this season which typifies life here. A competition exists on the Isle of Man called the Railway Cup, presented by the Isle of Man Steam Railway Company (circa 1824), which is so large that when it's full of ale it's too heavy to lift to your mouth on your own. In order to win this competition the team has to finish in the top four by Christmas or the halfway stage of the season, 12 League games. The top four teams go into the hat to produce semi-finals and ultimately a Final on New Year's Day – not the most sensible of days for a football Final, amateur or professional. Once again the freakish Manx weather turned the Bowl (IoM Wembley, but actually a dump) into a mallard's playground, and the game was thankfully postponed. I don't think Peel would stand much chance playing soccer on a public holiday because of the enthusiasm of the previous evening's entertainment. The nightmare rains continued for three months, preventing us from playing any games at all. In fact, we went four months without a League game, the sort of thing that only happens when a country goes to war. The pressure mounted. We just had to win this trophy, the public expected it, and my critics were waiting to pounce. Even though it was widely accepted that I had done my catalyst job for Peel since I arrived, helping us to gain promotion by winning the second division championship, the FA Cup and the Hospital Cup, the jury was still out. My abilities as a manager were being examined and I could sense the vultures hovering. A similarity between professional and amateur football is that, attached to every club in every city or town in the world, negative bastards exist. One bloke told me that although I might know about English pro football, I didn't know or understand a thing about Manx football. I'm afraid these tossers do exist, and you've just got to be a bit thick-skinned. You certainly wouldn't leave these types of idiot in charge, though it's tempting to do so to see what sort of cluster f**k they make of it. The punters did have a right to be sceptical, though: the outstanding success in the 1996–97 season could be said to have had nothing to do with me and, like the pros, I had to be judged on results.

The Railway Cup Final eventually got played and ended 1–1, although if it had been the proverbial boxing match we'd have been declared winners after 20 minutes. The replay was scheduled for Saturday 30 January. On the Friday I had finally worked my notice at the local hospital, which was a day of celebration and some sadness. I always hate terminating relationships, no matter how tenuous, unless she's particularly hard work. Following the exchange of gifts and pleasantries in the staff room we headed off to a wine hostelry in Douglas called Bar George. I invited all the colleagues that I had had the pleasure of insulting over the last two years and we got stuck into some Argentinian red wine. The evening roared on and we reached Peel several sheets to the wind, ready for an evening's hooliganism. Things began to get out of control when I decided to order some Chinese food at around 10pm. I staggered around at 11pm like a semi-anaesthetised yak to discover in jaw-clanging amazement (not to mention the other punters in there) that I had ordered a full banquet for six people at 10pm – and at 10.15pm, 10.30pm and 10.45pm – or so they reckoned. The price was £135. It was such a huge order that it was presented to me by the owner and chef together, who then escorted me from the premises with my large cardboard box shaking me by the hand.

Returning to the Royal I was greeted with riotous laughter at the size of the portion of grub, which seemed to confirm what they'd suspected for a long time now – that I liked my food and was in effect a fat bastard. Kelvin, Maurice Powell, my two American students, Dan and Lance, and myself managed to wade through about £50 of the stuff. The remainder I rehoused and stashed in the back beer fridge in the garage. Keeping this amount of food cool was probably the reason why the thing packed in a few days ago. Nor was it easy keeping it quiet from the dragon, but somehow I managed. I came around on Saturday at about 11am convinced that it was bell-ringing time in at Canterbury Cathedral in my head. It was an empty, transient day, and I occupied my time wandering around Peel like an American tourist.

The replay was a great triumph. I had to play (not my policy as manager), but I thought it was a good idea as I'd had the ideal preparation – two gallons of Guinness and a £135 takeaway – so if anything, I had over-prepared. The game was unfortunately marred by some mindless thuggery by the opposition. We'd had a run-in with this particular lot 18 months earlier after Tom Clucas, ginger Peel legend, had rifled in the winner on 120 minutes in the Hospital Cup Final. This was an aptly named competition, as the brawl which followed, the like of which I'd never seen, put the local Accident and Emergency department on red alert. Maybe, I was thinking, that bloke was right – perhaps I didn't know about Manx football. A similar thing happened here following our 2–0 victory – Kelvin was pelted by stones by the opposition (not their fans – they don't have any) and I was hit with a losers' medal, which I promptly gave to a young Peel fan, who disappeared with it. To my utter amazement, the nutter who propelled the missile came to ask me where the f**k his f**king medal was during the post-match radio interview. I told him to catch a bus to Peel, if he dared, and start asking around.

Following the game I was invited to say a few words to the fans back in the club house at Peel by the president, Mike Richards. The celebrations had begun to hit full tilt by the time we got back there. The Peel populace does not need any encouragement when it comes to shifting a few, and the town had already removed the equivalent of Albania's national debt in alcohol by the time I arrived, head hardly fitting through the door, trophy in hand. It is an interesting talent the Manx have in that they would out-drink the Irish and French national drinking teams by a country mile given half the chance. About a year ago a survey declared the French the biggest consumers of alcohol in the world, each person consuming approximately 7.5 litres of pure alcohol per annum. The Irish and the Germans closely followed. Then I saw a survey in the local Manx rag which declared consumption figures of 15 litres.

Somewhat shocked, I could only muster a few words of thanks for the support and an invite back to my place for a bit of supper later on. For the evening's festivities I had made a schoolboy error and not organised a babysitter, and my wife had arranged to go out with her well-to-do opera socialites, so I had to press-gang Jen Bailey, our work's secretary (she prefers to be called 'practice manager') and all-round good gal, into minding the raptors for me. I rejoined the fray in the Whitehouse Inn at 7.30pm, where the celebrations were in full swing. Obviously, I had the next day off, having left the hospital on Friday, and so for the first time since I'd arrived on the rock I could celebrate without having to wander around in a trance at the hospital. I could lie in bed or wander the streets or even hit the golf course.

There it was, the largest and most expensive trophy in Europe, and we were hawking it around the pubs of Peel in time-honoured fashion. Apparently, the trophy had in previous years ended up in at the bottom of the harbour, while in a separate incident the lid amazingly found its way into the deep fat fryer in the local chip shop. It was a worry to me in that, given the history, we were entrusted with this piece of silverware, this piece of Manx heritage, valued at £60,000 but with an actual remake or replace value of £250,000. When the cup is full of ale and other hallucinatory ingredients you have to employ the help of two beer-drinking assistants in order to imbibe the victory slurp. The evening descended into a night at the degenerates' ball, and most people made the pilgrimage back to the Royal for the last five hours.

I was suddenly struck down with another bout of Chinese-related amnesia and went to order another £40 worth of monosodium glutamate. I must have reminded everyone in the pub that the debacle was to continue back at my place, and I then I staggered out of the Royal into the depths of the Peel night. My first port of call was Rick Wakeman's music emporium, which had recently been painted a garish yellow, but I didn't care what colour it was as long as it did its job of holding me reasonably upright. At this very moment, or so the story goes, my wife was driving along the adjacent street engaged in a full-blown discussion about the sins of debauchery, particularly concerning alcoholics. 'Of course, Peel's full of them,' said Jean's well-to-do mate. 'And what's more, I hear they won the Cup today so they'll all be out tonight. It's pathetic.' As the car entered Atholl Place, named after the Dukes of Atholl, a dark figure was perceived leaning up against the aforementioned rock star's building like a wounded soldier in what physios would call slump standing, armed once again with a Chinese. 'Look, there's one over there and he's wearing a hat and – oh my God – he's being sick now.' I must confess that I couldn't cope with the volume anymore and opted for my trusty technique, which I had perfected all those years ago while drinking for my college, of the old inverted 'V' sign into the throat and out with all the contents. It was a garish yellow and set off the building quite well. At this point Jean recognised the forlorn figure to be yours truly and put her foot down in panic to avoid embarrassment. Five minutes later I had advanced about as far as the British Army in 1916 in northern France, and what I needed was a trench or a bullet. Suddenly the hum of Jean's Volvo penetrated my senses, and before I knew it I was bundled into the back seat and driven off like some kind of high-speed getaway from a bank job. Two minutes later I was ejected from the vehicle outside our front door like a dead body after a gangland killing, and then the car sped off. Jen, the long-suffering babysitter, let me in, and apparently after rugby-tackling her I slipped into the kitchen and set out the Chinese for the visitors. They duly arrived and a huge banquet along the lines of Henry VIII was undertaken with gluttonous fervour.

The following morning I came round at about 7am, woken by the raptors, and expected another hangover to kick in. Strangely, I felt fine. I flung back the curtains to be greeted by a very clement February morn. The sea was millpond calm and as blue as the sky. I located the wife in a spare room – my snoring had obviously got the better of her again – but she seemed none the worse for the ordeal. The kitchen floor was like a skating rink, awash with Chinese remnants which had left a grease slick more or less everywhere. There was that unmistakable post-house party stench of stale ale and smoke emanating from the half-finished drinks and full ash trays. This was going to take some tidying, and I couldn't rope the other lads in. I was faced with it myself. There, in the middle of it all, was Mingan, sitting faithfully aloof yet unfazed by it. He'd seen it all before. Nothing had really changed in the last 12 years, only the location and a few people.

It had occurred to me when we were driving back to Peel the previous night, as I gazed out at this new found landscape and contemplated my existence, that, despite everything, I'd survived. I'd found a happy ending in a strange sort of paradise. I had a lovely house and three healthy children, and my pal Jean was still hanging in there. I wasn't skint like I used to be in the old days and I had my health. And being so far west you're always driving towards a serene light, a marvellous sunset which offers hope and prosperity, and a warmth and sense of belonging. I'd always wanted to live as far west as I could in the British Isles – I harboured an unhealthy distrust of the east – and here I was, almost before I knew it. What I'd been through was now only the beginning, though. I was going to slow down and preserve life.

We all know, however, that this is impossible, and there were other things to achieve for Peel. In the next few months, we won the other two Cups, the Manx FA Cup and the Hospital Cup. Sadly we missed out on the Grand Slam and came runners-up in the League. We put that right in 2000 but, as is often the case, at the expense of the Cup competitions. We won the League for the first time in 16 years, a great achievement which was celebrated to the maximum.

There was still something to achieve for the Isle of Man, though. For the last seven years the island had been playing in an amateur knock-out cup against the Republic of Ireland, Northern Ireland and Scotland. Results had improved year on year, but there still hadn't been a win. I had been the senior coach for the last two competitions. In the year 2000 we hosted the competition, called the Guinness Cup, and I'll proudly announce that, as the national coach of the team, it was tremendous to win the Cup on home soil. We humbled the Scots in the Final 2–0 and we got the tactics spot on. These are the amateur internationals, and for the island to win it is similar to Uruguay beating Argentina, Brazil and Chile in terms of population and players to choose from. I had used that very angle to get my men up on a psychological pitch, and it worked. We played hard and gave the visitors a hard time. To say that they were sick is an underestimation, and to say that myself, the manager Kevin Manning, and the boys were delighted is an even bigger underestimation. A huge celebration was had. Starting from such a long way back in terms of resources made these amateur successes almost amazing. I was up there to fail and lots of people were in the background waiting for me to fail. Call me paranoid, but since my early childhood I had always been told that I wouldn't make it. Just look at my last school report. People want to pull you down. Look at that letter from the GP in Halifax. I have not been popular with a certain few since arriving on the island for whatever reason, be it jealousy, things I have said, or that I am English. I have had the last laugh, though, and have been successful and had great fun at the same time. No one can argue with the results. Don't get me wrong, lots of nice people were delighted that we won and quite a few have congratulated me directly, though I am sad to say that those who didn't therefore stand out even more. Yet despite everything, you've got to keep going. The goal posts have moved in my life yet again and new challenges await. Time for a change.

# nine

## In the End

I had left the hospital's mundane environment and worked with Adrian before branching out on my own. By now it was June 2002 and the World Cup. Peel had just won the League for the third consecutive time and we decided to throw a huge party, or rather I did. This was such a debacle that my wife kicked me out, but despite it all we have remained good friends and the children have thrived on the rock. Contrary to popular belief, I did not simply choose to live in a campervan on Peel prom, but I did buy one to take the kids out in. I carried on working hard at my physio practice, with Peel AFC and at being Dad.

Things were looking up, but I felt the need to get a new and final challenge as there was still something missing in the jigsaw. I evaluated it thus: normal childhood and gone to a boys' rugby-playing grammar school and eventually to university; a degree and a football career involving rising to play at the top level in the country and another degree; marriage and three children; the running of an outpatient physiotherapy department in a hospital, and then starting my own business; a successful management and coaching career at amateur level with Peel and the Isle of Man team, divorce and then starting financially again. What next?

In July 2004 I was busy away at the clinic when my secretary told me that Andy Ritchie had phoned and that he wanted an urgent reply. It transpired that he was at Barnsley FC as the assistant to manager Paul Hart and that the physio had run away from the club at the last minute and left them in the lurch for the coming tour of

France – could I fill in? Too right, I thought. I could do with a holiday, and to make a few quid at the same time was ideal. Without hesitation I got myself organised and shot over to Barnsley the following day as they were due to depart the day after. In my excitement I forgot to mention it to anyone, including the girl that I had been going out with for some time, and when I rang her from Bordeaux it went down like a burning Messerschmitt. It dawned on me during the tour, which was a typical pre-season debacle (nothing had changed since my days), that this would be a great opportunity to get back into the game. I had missed my chance to do it by turning Sunderland down in 2000, and when I was offered the full-time post by Peter Ridsdale, I jumped at the chance. This was the opportunity to complete the loop.

I quickly got to grips with the job and proved to one and all that I was your proper bonkers physio, and I hit it off with the players and staff. I warmed to Paul Hart instantly and loved his despairing dry, doom-laden sense of humour. His reaction when I returned after being sent for some red wine to a hypermarché in Soulac with Chilean wine will live with me till the day I pop off. His approach to the lads was different and I learned pretty quickly that he was good mates with Steve Harrison of my Watford days, as they had been at Blackpool together back in the seventies, and their styles were very similar. Both are excellent coaches, but their man-management styles were sometimes a little hard and fraught. On the surface it seemed a happy club, full of energy and ambition, and when we returned to Barnsley I could see that the facilities demanded success. What a change from the dour past that I had come to know and hate. There was something not quite right coming down from the top, however, and I could quite clearly see tension between the owner's clique and the chairman's clique, which included the management. Peter Ridsdale clearly puts the manager and his players first and trusts his managers completely. The same was not to be said for the owner's lot. Although they will claim passion for the club, they did not seem to have the same passion for the management and the players. I could be wrong, but this was the vibe.

I didn't have any trouble fitting in with the south Yorkies. I am, after all, a Yorkshireman, albeit from a totally different part of Yorkshire. Norman Rimmington, the evergreen Barnsley stalwart, pulled me one morning and said in his 80-odd-year-old thick Barnsley accent, 'Eee lad, thas a rum bugger thee.' Yep, he had sussed me out and I had sussed them out. It was respect. They had all remembered me playing for teams in the enemy county of Lancashire and the damage that I had meted out to them at times. I decided to live up in west Yorkshire in Cullingworth, which is next door to the world-famous Haworth, where the Brontë family lived. My sister, on returning from the rock after three years of Manx life due to cabin fever, had persuaded my dad to buy a small cottage. It was a lucky purchase in hindsight and saved a fortune. I eventually bought my sister and my dad out of the place and, with the help of my sister, Jen, did the shit-hole up.

So I had returned home to Yorkshire where I had been born and raised. I had guessed that this was going to be it now, as they don't tend to sack physios in the game much, and this was destiny in that I was a footballing man and this was my life. Even Ann, my girlfriend, tolerated the long-distance relationship and thoroughly enjoyed the trips over. The downside was that I missed the kids terribly and made hundreds of trips back to the island to see them and Ann. This was expensive and time-consuming, but worth it. I was living a dual life.

Things had changed in Yorkshire in some respects, and yet in others they hadn't. The M62 was now the busiest road on the planet in a morning, and to get to work for Harty's regimen meant setting off at 6am for an 8.30am start, travelling a distance of only 45 miles, mostly on the motorway. Other things, like my mates' movements back home in Embsay, hadn't changed one jot. I could still work out where they would be at any given time of the day or week.

I settled into life and bumped into a few old acquaintances including, incredibly, the renegade linesman who had tried to get me sent off at Barnsley. I was rehabilitating a few players in the Brooklands Hotel swimming pool when in he came and plunged into the jacuzzi with a knowing smile, as if reliving his glory moment. I returned the nod of acknowledgement and he knew. On the pitch we had the makings of a good team, but they seemed devoid of luck and I also detected fatigue. The away trips were funny events in which Paul and Peter ensured that the players had the best of accommodation, relaxation and food, and so did we. Once the lads had been settled, all the staff were ordered to meet in the gaffer's room for pre-meal drinks and I continued the Chilean wine saga, much to the despair of Paul and the amusement of Andy and company. The evening would rage on and the discussions on football would become heated, and everyone including Peter would put their two-pennyworth in. I would then get sacked and Harty would storm off. The following morning the phone would ring at about 9am and it would be Harty: 'You're reinstated! Get down here with some headache tablets please.'

Equally funny were some of the dressing-room rants at half-times. Some of the best and funniest bollockings that I have ever seen and heard were delivered by Harty during this period, the best being Swindon away, where his one-liners reduced me to tears of laughter. I had to hide round the corner in the shower area to avoid detection. Lines like, 'Can anyone tell me what the f**k is going on out there?' and 'I've seen some things out there today that I have never seen in my life before and things that I didn't think were f**king possible on a football pitch.' I think he was referring to Tom Williams's attempted clearance from left-back to a left-wing Swindon cross, which he'd put four yards over his own crossbar.

The players' performances didn't help him, but his anxiety from the pressure didn't help them and I am sure led to some of the unbelievable pieces of anti-skill that we witnessed during this half of the season. Tony Vaughan's mistake at Hartlepool summed it up. For some reason, when chasing a ball which was just innocuously plonked into the channel as a sort of clearance, Tony answered it by giving chase, sliding on his arse and then crossing it into the box for their centre-forward to run on to and bury in to the back of the net. There was no accounting for this behaviour other than collective stress.

Things had started to go wrong for me too. What started as a great idea in running my clinic with a locum suddenly backfired when the lad I had got in from Hull, called Tony, revealed that he had a suspended jail sentence from a dose of air rage, and the Chartered Society of Physiotherapy had suspended him for 18 months. I ended up supporting a non-functioning clinic with the salary that Barnsley was paying me. I was hiring myself out to Barnsley as a consultant of my own business anyway, which I could do for a year, taking advantage of an agreement called the 90-night rule. This was allowed to be lumped together into one long year in four, so I was knackered after that and would have to become an employee of Barnsley in the summer of 2005 anyway. Then worse – Ann arrived to look at the prospect of living with me, but it coincided with a tragic bit of news. Tommy Clucas, my mate and centre-forward partner in the first monumental season at Peel, crashed and died while ahead in the Manx Grand Prix in early September 2004. He had just broken the lap record of 120mph average speed for the 37-mile course on the third lap and had spilled due to engine seizure at Ballaugh Bridge. This set me off and Ann cleared off to Hull to her brother's place.

There was then a takeover at Barnsley, which dislodged Peter Ridsdale and Dave Walker and replaced them with Gordon Shepherd, a one-time part-time director, and saw the owner take a more hands-on role. The writing was on the wall from this moment. It's like the law of the jungle when a new male lion takes over the pride and then proceeds to kill all the lion cubs because they aren't his. In football, when a new manager comes in, he usually ditches all those that he feels will stab him in the back and then brings his own backroom staff in with him. It's the same at director and chairman level, only it's more a case of bringing in people they can control and getting rid of dangerous radicals like me. What they do is buy themselves time with the fans, so they keep the insurgents in position for a while. No point sacking the gaffer and staff if they are not in a perilous League position. Best off doing things by stealth, which is what they did. I was summoned to Shepherd's office, where he promptly sacked me, saying that I was on too much money and they were making cutbacks. I was just about to walk out and then something he said made me check my stride. He had asked me what I would do, could I coach or something? Clearly he didn't have a clue who I was and what my qualifications were. I asked him if he knew who I was and he just looked at me and did a peculiar thing with his head, sort of nodding it and shaking it at the same time. I informed him that I had done x, y and z and then watched him crank his chin up off the floor. He had just thought that I was some ordinary sponge-bag bloke without any football history. He then said that he would think about it.

Harty, Andy Ritchie and I went to a pub on the way to Doncaster somewhere and talked about the future, or the lack of it. We talked of the sack and the futility of football and why the hell we were in it. Paul was still respected by the lads and they played japes on us all the time. One favourite was the covering over of Harty's rear number plate with physio tape, which got him pulled by the cops on the M1. He played along with it very well and said that he was going to get points on his license for it. Anthony Kay, who did it, was a little shocked for a while. Two days after our little chat in the pub, Harty was fired and Andy was given the caretaker manager's job. I was asked to step up to assistant manager and continue with the physio job too. The first job was to keep the team in League One, which was looking a bit shaky, but Andy quickly picked up the manager of the month award and we made it comfortably, rounding off the season with an away win at Blackpool. Some hilarious things happened during this little run-in, none funnier than an away win at runaway leaders Luton. Neil Austin, who was selected for the bench that day, came up to me and asked if I could strap his ankle before the game. This was strange as he never normally asked for this. Neil had been vying all season for the award of team clown, along with Michael Chopra, Nicky Wroe, Dale Tonge, Anthony Kay and Rob Williams. I took one look at his ankle and saw that it was swollen. I decided to give it a rub to get the swelling down and then strapped it and off he went to warm up. Bear in mind that this game was live on Sky TV on the Easter Friday. During the warm-up Ozzy started to limp and the fans evidently saw this as it was later reported back to me by Craig Savage, a mate and Barnsley fan who was watching it on the big screen in Barnsley or 'Tarn' as they call it. At half-time we walked across the pitch from the dug-outs. Ozzy was clearly limping now, and I could see Andy's face looking bemused. He didn't say anything – we were winning. During the second half Ozzy called to me and said it was getting worse. Andy then instructed me to get Ozzy on the pitch as a substitute. Ozzy said that he couldn't go on. 'What the f**k's up with Ozzy?' said the gaffer. I replied that I didn't have a clue but that he couldn't go on. After the game we did the same walk across the pitch, only this time Ozzy had to be chaired by two of the lads.

The same 'What the f**k has happened to him?' thought must have been going through all the fans, press and directors' minds, as surely we wouldn't put an injured player on the bench? It turned out that he had been kicked by one of the lads in training on the Tuesday but didn't want to mention it as he thought he could get away with it. I had irritated it when I massaged it and must have caused the thing to rebleed. What a showing up, but very funny all the same – a player gets injured on the bench! It's a good job we won.

It was a constant problem getting the lads to tell the whole truth as by and large they all want to play, especially if they are on appearance money. I had the same with Rob Williams when we played Manchester City in the League Cup at Eastlands. By half-time we were getting battered, and Rob was getting roasted by Wright-Phillips. He couldn't run and Harty went spare with me for not telling him that Rob was struggling with his groin. Rob hadn't told me, so what was I supposed to do? Rob confessed and apologised, but he didn't want to miss the chance of playing in a big game and thought that he could get away with it. It is hard enough marking that lad when fully fit, never mind with a sore groin. In the Blackpool win, the club captain, Paul Reid, sat through the game in his suit because Swifty, the kit man, had forgotten to pack his gear. He was on the bench as a named player among the subs, and this again caused some raised eyebrows.

We retired for the summer, uncertain as to whether we were going to be asked to carry on with the job next season. Shepherd and the owner couldn't sack us as we were popular with the fans, the players and even the press. They were stuck with us, and I feel they reluctantly let us get on with the task of getting promotion, which I had informed the Wing Commander (the chairman, so named as during endless meetings he used to rattle on about his days flying in the RAF in the 1950s) it would be possible in one or two years. The chairman, secretary and owner were keen to run things as much as they could but they needed us. It still didn't stop them signing Richard Kell with a broken leg and Brian Howard without checking his medical notes. Howard had had a fifth metatarsal fracture previously without it being pinned. They never even informed me. I was then charged with trying to get them fit. Poor old Richard never made it back.

The season was helter-skelter and we played some great football. Everyone was pulling together, life was good again and I was even getting on well with Ann; we were engaged very shortly after. We made the play-offs and faced Swansea in the Final in

May 2006 at the Millennium Stadium, Cardiff. I had proved to myself that I could coach at professional level, and the things that I had implemented at Peel worked with the pros. Andy and I, with Tom Little's invaluable input as fitness coach and masseur, used a combination of old-world stuff from our playing days and the modern stuff, such as SAQ work, which stands for 'speed, agility, quickness'. The SAQ routines involve all sorts of equipment like hurdles. It worked a treat. I even altered the times of training in deep winter to try to maximise the benefits of sunlight to help avoid fatigue caused by SAD (Seasonal Affective Disorder) syndrome. It still didn't stop the chairman from dragging us to yet another endless afternoon meeting to ask us why the lads weren't doing 9 'til 5 like the man in the street. I had to inform him that we weren't up against the man in the street on Saturday.

D-Day arrived and we had some inside information from the groundsman on the Friday night about what footwear to use; he was obviously a Cardiff City fan and didn't want Swansea to win. We had to get some of the lads some new boots on the Saturday morning, and I ended up leaving my boots at the hotel so I had to use a pair of Paul Hayes's spare ones for assist and physio duties. We started well, scoring early, and then a nightmare howler from our 'keeper, Nick Colgan, and another goal meant we went in at half-time 2–1 down. This was my time, my finest hour. As I approached the dressing room Andy, Tom and Martin Wilkinson, the chief scout, were standing outside trying to sort things out. I knew what was required and said to the gaffer, 'Just let me sort it out.' The lads were down, and it was quite clear to me that what they needed was a psychological boost, not technical stuff. I quite simply told them to keep calm and that I knew what Kenny Jacket was thinking because I had played with him at Watford. I said that he would instruct his players to keep a clean sheet and then they would win. I told our mob that this was flawed thinking and that if we scored it would feel like losing to them and we would have the upper hand and go on to win. Of course this was somewhat made up as I didn't know what Kenny was saying, only that it is the best way to approach adversity in sport.

We did score and took it to extra-time and then the dreaded penalties. The penalties were in front of the Swansea fans, which was good for us. I had insisted on another thing, which was that in the two weeks prior to the Play-offs we practised penalties. I don't buy the argument that you can't practise penalties when people say that they are referring to the loss of nerve on the occasion. My argument is that if you have practised and you are confident about your technique then you can keep calm in the knowledge that you can put the ball where you want to. It's like standing on the 72 tee in a Major and you need to hit it down the middle to win the tournament. You have to shut the outside world out and rely on technique. It's the same if you have to shut out a delivery from the best bowler in the world to save the game. It is nerve, yes, but you need technique. This was no problem for the boys: four of the best penalties you could ever wish for. What's more, Swansea failed in their technique and blazed over. Nick Colgan became the hero and compensated for his earlier error by saving the final penalty, and he deserved it. We had done it: and I had done it proved to myself that I could succeed at pro level. I was a winner. It is there forever. Job done.

This didn't cut any mustard with the chairman and the owner, and we knew we were still going to be kicked out. It just made it more difficult for them to do it. The end was swift and poignant. The first blatant act of gross indecency was the sacking of Mick Tarmey, the academy manager, and replacing him with Simon Davy. Mick is a thoroughly decent man and would never let anyone down, and just as his wife was diagnosed with cancer, they cut his balls off. What made it worse was that they sacked him before the end of the season and even brought the snake to the end-of-season dinner dance. That's some people in football for you. Cast your mind back to my first manager, Tommy Cavanagh. It was obvious that Davy was brought in to spy on us and he would report things back to the chairman, which we found out by laying traps of crap information which got back to us. John Lukic, our goalkeeper coach, rumbled them, and he let them know. It wasn't rocket science, but it was pathetic. We made a great start to life in the Championship, even though we hadn't been given any money for players, and we were forced to let go of our best player, Stephen McPhail. It must have really hurt them when Andy got manager of the month again. Then we hit a sticky patch, but we were still being admired, not more so than by Sheffield Wednesday's chairman, who wanted permission to speak to Andy Ritchie. Andy and I had not been offered new contracts following promotion so we all knew we were up for the chop, and Sheffield Wednesday's chairman knew it. Shepherd refused permission for Andy to hold talks with Wednesday and publicly said that a new offer was on the table for Andy to sign. It then went quiet and there wasn't a contract for Andy. Then we were sacked, me for the second time. To no one's surprise, Davy was named as Barnsley manager. By the time I was sacked, I was head physio, assistant manager, first-team coach and reserve-team manager. The bastards had me doing a one-man-band act.

I returned home to my cottage and went out. The next day Ann informed me that it was all over, and it was all my fault. I went to the toilet but it was blocked. A young physio called Sharif, from the island, was staying with me as he had been helping out at Barnsley. He had blocked the f**king toilet. Then the boiler blew up so I didn't have any heating or hot water. I went into the back yard to have a dump. What else could I do? There I was, squatting over a newspaper, contemplating that I had a blocked toilet, a broken boiler, I had lost my job and lost my beautiful fiancée. How could things get worse? There was a loud crash in the sky and the heavens opened. Minging!

I packed up and returned to the rock, wondering what to do. I did nothing for a few weeks and eased my way back in with Peel by helping out on the coaching side. Chris Hawke was the manager but instantly asked me to do the job. We won the Railway Cup straight away, the first win since I was gaffer in 2003 when we had won the same Cup. I knew I could do the football stuff now, so it was no big deal. I had proved that. What of life though? I had to open the clinic up again and start earning some money, and I did this out of Peel football club. The deal was to be manager and to run the physio from there. It was great to be back with my family and friends again and away from the endless groundhog day of football. It gave me a chance to reflect on my life and what I had achieved, and on football and its ups and downs. I could try to recapture Ann, who was back on the rock, though the immediate chance I blew when I kidnapped her dog in a moment of madness.

Football has some smashing people but it is also the lurking ground of some really sinister, horrible people whom the game could do without. The proof is in my story, but I am not the only one with these experiences – just ask any pro footballer. It's the good guys that get it worse too: Dave Longhurst died in 1990, Mel Rees in 1993, Billy Ayre in 2002 and Tommy Clucas in 2005 – all great lads, and the good lads that survive keep getting shat upon too, Paul Hart again in 2009 by Portsmouth and Andy Ritchie in 2008 by Huddersfield. I was offered the assistant job at Huddersfield, but I took one look at it and turned it down as I knew they would sack Andy even though he was doing a good job.

I have maintained all along that this book is not about the specifics of the goings-on at the various clubs, but more about my life as I briefly passed through them. As I was shutting this journey down I started to think about the characters whom I had met and who had influenced me. I thought about Billy Ayre and Mick Jones, who got me going after the Burnley rejection. Without them I would have been just another lad who could have made it. I thought of Steve Harrison and Tom, who took a chance on me and elevated me from the Fourth Division to the First. Peter Reid and Sam Ellis were great, I had much fun with them, and when I look in detail it was a fantastic season with them at City. Sam used to send me off in training and tell me to come back in the afternoon, so I would go and do some individual work with Tony Book while Sam bored the tits off the lads with a training-ground routine. Then I would get a message from Sam to meet him in the Salutation, a favourite pub down the road from Platt Lane, where I would get my bollocking over a pint and then be sent on my way until the next time it happened. You wouldn't get that now – it's changed. I thought of Big Sam Allardyce and my maverick mate Phil Brown wrestling with their new-found toy of sports science, and I remembered how people took the piss out of me when I was telling them about the subject and its benefits to the game all the years before when I was studying it at Leeds.

I also thought about the peculiarities of the Blackpool stint and how they still believed in me, even if Sharpy didn't. I thought of Sharpy himself and why it didn't work and where I had gone wrong. I don't, on reflection, hold anything against him now. Then Joe and Willie at Oldham and the glory years come to mind, how Willie, with his off-the-map coaching ideas, wanted to make us all bigger, quicker, stronger, and how he used to go mad if we didn't buy into his ideas. There are so many Willie

Donachie stories but they will have to wait. Big Joe himself, the affable, intelligent northerner who allowed me to be me and perhaps had been the biggest single influence on my development. I thought of my early years with Mum, Dad and Jen, and finally Grandpa, who believed in me but couldn't believe it. I thank all these people and am grateful to have met them. Life was over now in this respect, and I have turned the page.

Writing these last few recollections sitting outside the creek, I was beginning to feel a bit down and sorry for myself, thinking what a minging life. I had done all these things and yet got nowhere, and I had lost the person who walked in that day in 2000 and would never see her again. But then I began to smile to myself and broke into a laugh. I had my health and my family. I had some great friends and I lived in a beautiful place. I had my own job and was my own boss. Never again was some idiot going to tell me what to do. I had proved all my doubters wrong from my earliest days up until the last few months. I have not been back to Barnsley since and I believe that they do not display any pictures of me or Andy and our glory. We are the first to actually win anything since 1912, and that can never be taken away from us. I was a winner, and a little flower had just arrived on the scene. As the sun danced on the harbour waters of Peel, I raised my glass and made a toast. It wasn't such a minging life after all.